Plant-Bas

Cookboo

Yummy

Plant Based-Diet Receipes To Lose Weight, Boost Brain Health & Reverse Disease.

Table of Contents

Glossary Of Cooking Terms

BASTE

To moisten foods during cooking with pan drippings or special sauce to add flavor and prevent drying.

BATTER

A mixture containing flour and liquid, thin enough to pour.

BEAT

To mix rapidly in order to make a mixture smooth and light by incorporating as much air as possible.

BOIL

To heat a liquid until bubbles break continually on the surface.

BROIL

To cook on a grill under strong, direct heat.

CHOP

To cut solids into pieces with a sharp knife or other chopping device.

DEGLAZE

To dissolve the thin glaze of juices and brown bits on the surface of a pan in which food has been fried, sauteed or roasted. To do this, add liquid and stir and scrape over high heat, thereby adding flavor to the liquid for use as a sauce.

DICE

To cut food in small cubes of uniform size and shape.

DRIZZLE

To sprinkle drops of liquid lightly over food in a casual manner.

FLAKE

To break lightly into small pieces.

FRY

To cook in hot fat. To cook in a fat is called pan-frying or sauteing; to cook in a one-to-two inch layer of hot fat is called shallow-fat frying; to cook in a deep layer of hot fat is called deep-fat frying.

GARNISH

To decorate a dish both to enhance its appearance and to provide a flavorful foil. Parsley, lemon slices, raw vegetables, chopped chives, and other herbs are all forms of garnishes.

GRATE

To rub on a grater that separates the food in various sizes of bits or shreds.

GRATIN

From the French word for "crust." Term used to describe any oven-baked dish--usually cooked in a shallow oval gratin dish--on which a golden brown crust of bread crumbs, cheese or creamy sauce is form.

GRILL

To cook on a grill over intense heat.

GRIND

To process solids by hand or mechanically to reduce them to tiny particles.

KNEAD

To work and press dough with the palms of the hands or mechanically, to develop the gluten in the flour.

MINCE

To cut or chop food into extremely small pieces.

MIX

To combine ingredients usually by stirring.

PEEL

To remove the peels from vegetables or fruits.

PICKLE

To preserve meats, vegetables, and fruits in brine.

PUREE

To mash foods until perfectly smooth by hand, by rubbing through a sieve or food mill, or by whirling in a blender or food processor.

SAUTE

To cook and/or brown food in a small amount of hot fat.

SIMMER

To cook slowly in liquid over low heat at a temperature of about 180°. The surface of the liquid should be barely moving, broken from time to time by slowly rising bubbles.

STIR

To mix ingredients with a circular motion until well blended or of uniform consistency.

Introduction

A plant based diet is a diet where you only consume natural foods which the ground produces. Therefore anything that you eat must be in its natural and unprocessed form whenever possible. Most raw food dieters eat their foods in their raw state because they contain more nutrients than cooked foods.

In recent years, adopting a plant-based diet has become increasingly popular, as it has benefits for our bodies and for the planet. With this lifestyle, you will be taking advantage of whole foods of plant origin to nourish your body optimally. You will also leave a smaller environmental footprint, as sustainable eating habits can help reduce greenhouse gas emissions, in addition to the consumption of water and land used for industrial agriculture.

Chapter 1

Plant-Based Diet: A Diet to Reverse Heart Disease

The primary causes for chronic illnesses such as heart disease and diabetes are biochemical and physiological imbalances. These imbalances are mostly due to the unnatural, processed foods that we are putting in our bodies. As long as we continue to eat the wrong foods, it doesn't matter how much we spend on health care, we will still be getting sick.

Heart disease is the leading cause of death in the United States. On a global scale, about 452 million people die each year from this condition. The sad fact behind these deaths is that they are mostly preventable. With the proper nutrition, this condition can not only be prevented, but reversed.

Exercise is often extolled as a preventative measure for heart disease. While exercise is very important to health and wellbeing, it is not the most critical factor. Many people who suffer from high cholesterol, obesity, hypertension and diabetes still have these conditions even when they are following a regular program of exercise. The benefits from exercise alone are not sufficient for preventing heart disease, diabetes and the long list of other chronic illnesses that afflict our society.

There has been much emphasis placed on nutrition and its role in prevention. The problem is that there is often a lack of understanding about what constitutes proper nutrition.

Counting calories and monitoring fat, protein and carbohydrate intake is not going to prevent heart disease. It's not just the number of calories, carbohydrates or fat you're taking in that matter. It comes down to the nature and quality of the food.

A natural, whole foods, plant-based diet has been shown to prevent and reverse heart disease. Experts have shown extensive scientific evidence on how animal-based foods contribute to chronic conditions such as heart disease and diabetes. There are many examples of patients who have cured themselves of heart disease simply by eliminating animal products and other unhealthy substances from their diet.

In addition to removing animal products from the diet, it is also important to cut out all unnatural substances. Artificial ingredients and processed foods have chemicals that do a significant amount of damage to the body. A food, such as an apple that was originally healthy becomes unhealthy after it has been processed into some other product.

When you take out all processed foods and artificial ingredients and abstain from eating animal products, you are left with only the most nutritious foods in your diet. Fresh fruits and vegetables have a high concentration of vitamins, minerals, enzymes and phytochemicals. All of this substances work together harmoniously in ways that modern science still does not completely understand. Our technology cannot surpass the engineering of nature to provide us with the best possible nutrition.

When we as a society learn how to eat for optimal health, we will see drastic reductions in chronic illnesses and their related costs. We do not need to live in fear of heart disease. Once we change our lifestyle and eating habits and follow the proper guidelines for nutrition, we can eliminate this illness and enjoy far greater health.

Chapter 2
Why Consider a Plant-Based Diet?

1. Weight Loss

One of the great benefits of the plant based diet is weight loss. This diet will not only help you to lose weight and fat cells, but all that cellulite which no one seems to be able to get rid of, will also begin to disappear.

2. Prevent Cancer

A plant based diet can also protect you against all types of cancers. This is because most plants are high in antioxidants which help the body to get rid of toxins which cause the cells in your body to become cancerous.

3. Boost Immune System

Did you know that about 80% of your immune system is situated in your digestive system? Thus if your digestive system is clogged, then your immune system will be down and you will be susceptible to all kinds of diseases and common ailments.

Plants are high in fiber, and when it passes through your digestive system, it latches on to all the gunk that has built up along the sides of your intestinal wall and eliminates it from the body. Once all this buildup is removed from your body, your immune system can function normal again and protect you against allergies, the common cold and autoimmune disorders such as HIV.

4. Fights Diabetes

A plant based diet does not spike your blood sugar levels as many other conventional foods do. Therefore you will never have to worry about diabetes.

5. Anti-Aging

The diet also helps to protect you from the free radicals that contribute to aging. According to studies, free radicals are the number one cause of aging both internally and externally. Therefore the diet can help you to avoid age related diseases, and keep you looking and feeling young. But not only will the diet protect your physical being, but your mind will also be able to remain young and strong.

6. Lowers Cholesterol Naturally

 When you consume raw fruits and veggies you do not have to worry about high cholesterol. However, when you consume a diet rich in meat you have a great chance of contracting a case of high cholesterol. Here is why. Meats are high in fat and fat plays a major role in high cholesterol. Plants have little to no fat so you will merely glean nutrients. Some meat eaters switch to a low-fat diet and fail to see lower cholesterol results. They fail to understand that a low-fat diet is of no value unless the meat is eliminated or significantly reduced. Your liver loves plants because it does not have to work as hard to regulate the cholesterol. ⬜

Chapter 3: Plant-Based Break Fast Recipes

Apricot Overnight Oats

Serves 4

Total Time 5 min

Ingredients

- 2 cups gluten-free rolled oats

- ¼ cup apricot preserves
- 2¼ cups non-dairy milk
- 2 apples
- 3 tbsp goji berries
- ½ cup macadamia nuts
- 2 tbsp cashew butter

Instructions

- In a large bowl or container with a lid, combine the oats, apricot preserves, non-dairy milk, and a pinch of salt. Cover and refrigerate overnight or for at least 8 hours.
- Divide the overnight oats into 4 servings. When you're ready to eat, dice the apples. Layer the following on top of each serving: diced apples, goji berries, macadamia nuts, and cashew butter

Avocado Toasts With Roma Tomatoes

Serves 2

Total Time 5 min

Ingredients

- 4 slices sourdough bread
- 2 Roma tomatoes
- 2 avocados
- ¼ cup vegan basil pesto
- ¼ cup balsamic glaze

Instructions

- Toast the bread. Thinly slice the tomatoes. Halve the avocados and remove the pits.
- Scoop half of an avocado onto each piece of toast and mash with a fork. Top the avocado toast with pesto and sliced tomatoes. Drizzle with balsamic glaze.

Yogurt Bowls Recipe

Serves 4

Total Time 5 min

Ingredients

- 4 kiwis
- 8 oz Purely Elizabeth Ancient Grain Granola
- 10.6 oz Vanilla Forager Project Cashewgurt
- ¼ cup goji berries

Instructions

- Peel and dice the kiwis.
- Divide the granola between 4 bowls.
- Top with Cashewgurt, diced kiwis, and goji berries.

Superfood Toasts With Hemp Seeds & Goji Berries

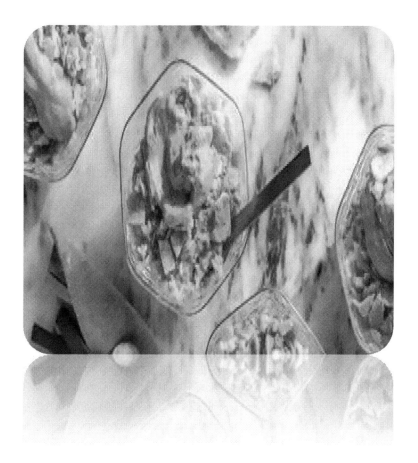

Serves 3

Total Time 7 min

Ingredients

- 4 whole wheat English muffins
- ¼ cup pistachios
- ¼ cup almond butter

- ¼ cup goji berries
- 2 tbsp hemp seeds
- 2 agave packet

Instructions

- Toast as many of the english muffins as you'd like. Roughly chop the pistachios.
- Evenly spread the almond butter on the toasted bread. Top with pistachios, hemp seeds, and goji berries.
- Drizzle with agave.

Overnight Oats Made With Peanut Butter

Serves 2

Total Time 5 min

Ingredients

- 2 cups gluten-free rolled oats
- 2 tbsp agave
- 2¼ cups non-dairy milk
- 2 oz dried figs

- 5.3 oz cup Forager Project Organic Vanilla Cashewgurt
- 2 tbsp cacao nibs
- ¼ cup peanut butter

Instructions

Make the oats the night before

- In a large bowl or container with a lid, combine the oats, agave, non-dairy milk, and a pinch of salt. Cover and refrigerate the oats overnight or for at least 8 hours.
- Divide the overnight oats into 4 serving dishes. When you are ready to eat, thinly slice the dried figs. Top with Cashewgurt, dried figs, cacao nibs, and peanut butter.

Granola Bowls Spirulina Recipe

Serves 3

Total Time 5 min

Ingredients

- 1 mango
- 2 tsp spirulina
- 12 oz Purely Elizabeth Ancient Grain Granola
- ¼ cup toasted coconut
- 4 cups non-dairy milk

Instructions

- Peel and dice the mango. Add the non-dairy milk and spirulina to a blender and blend on high until smooth.
- Divide the granola between 4 serving dishes.
- Top with diced mango and toasted coconut and pour in spirulina milk.

Apple Pie Overnight Oats With Marple Syrup

Serves 2

Total Time 10 min

Ingredients

- 2 red apples
- 2 cups gluten-free rolled oats
- ¼ cup maple syrup
- ½ tsp ground cinnamon
- 2¼ cups non-dairy milk

- 4 oz Purely Elizabeth Ancient Grain Granola
- 2 tbsp cashew butter

Instructions

- Dice the apples. In a bowl or container with a lid, combine the diced apples,oats, maple syrup, cinnamon, non-dairy milk, and a pinch of salt. Cover and refrigerate the oats overnight or at least 8 hours.
- Divide the overnight oats into 4 serving dishes. When you're ready to eat, top with ancient grain granola and cashew butter.

Break Fast Carrot Cake Smoothie Recipe

Serve 4

Total Time 6 min

Ingredients

- 2 oranges
- 6 oz shredded carrots
- 4 oz Purely Elizabeth Ancient Grain Granola
- 2 5.3 oz Forager Project Organic Cashewgurt

Instructions

Prepare the smoothies

- I recommend making 2 or 4 servings at a time and dividing the ingredients accordingly.
- Peel and deseed the oranges. In a blender, combine the oranges, shredded carrots, Cashewgurt, granola (saving a pinch to top the smoothies if you'd like), and 1 to 2 ice cubes per serving. Blend until smooth.
- Divide between glasses and top with any reserved granola.

Banana Foster Chia Pudding Recipe

Serves 2

Total Time 5 min

Ingredients

- ¾ cup chia seeds
- 5.5 oz coconut milk
- ¼ cup maple syrup

- ½ cup diced banana chips
- 2 oz Ceylon cinnamon crunch
- 2 cups non-dairy milk

Instructions

For chia seed pudding

- In a large bowl or container with a lid, combine the chia seeds, coconut milk, and non-dairy milk. Cover and refrigerate overnight or for at least 8 hours.
- Divide the chia seed pudding between 4 serving dishes. Drizzle with maple syrup.
- Sprinkle with banana chips and Ceylon cinnamon crunch.

Toasted Coconut Chia Parfait Recipe

Seves 3

Total Time 10 min

Ingredients

- ½ cup chia seeds
- 1 mango
- 10.6 oz Forager Project Vanilla Cashewgurt
- 4 oz Purely Elizabeth™ Ancient Grain Granola
- ½ cup toasted coconut
- 2 tbsp cashew butter

- 2 tbsp cacao nibs
- 1½ cups cups non-dairy milk

Instructions

For chia seed pudding

- In a bowl or a container with a lid, combine the chia seeds, milk, and a pinch of salt. Whisk well. Cover and refrigerate overnight or for at least 8 hours.
- Divide the chia seed pudding into 4 serving dishes. When you're ready to eat, peel and dice the mango.
- Layer the following on top of each chia seed pudding serving: yogurt, diced mango, granola, and coconut flakes. Top the parfaits with cashew butter and cacao nibs.

Borracho Beans

Prep Time: 10 minutes

Cooking Time: 60 minutes

Serves 6

Borracho beans are pinto beans that have been cooked with peppers, onion and tomatoes! You can try these beans with Mexican rice and flour tortillas.

Ingredients

- 6 cups cooked pinto beans and liquid
- 1 large tomato, diced
- 1 medium onion (preferably sweeter varieties like Walla Walla or Vidalia), diced
- 3 to 6 Serrano peppers (depending how picoso/spicy you want it), diced
- 1 bunch of cilantro, chopped

Directions

- Add the pinto beans, onion, tomato, and chiles into a medium-large pot and bring to a boil over medium heat. Reduce heat and allow to cook for 45 minutes at a rapid simmer, stirring often.
- Lower heat, add chopped cilantro, and allow to simmer on low for 15 minutes.
- Serve and enjoy!

Ceviche

Prep Time : 45 minutes

Cooking Time: 0 minutes

6 servings

Ceviche is a perfect and refreshing summer dish!

Ingredients

- 1 cauliflower, small-medium head
- 2 cups tomatoes, small dice
- 1 cup red onion, small dice
- 1 cup cilantro, chopped
- 1 cup cucumber, small dice
- ½ cup fresh lime juice
- 1 chile serrano (if you like it spicy you can add more)
- 1 teaspoon salt
- 1 teaspoon fresh black pepper
- 1 tablespoon ketchup
- Tostadas
- 2 avocados, pits removed, sliced

Directions

- In a large bowl, shred cauliflower with large-hole side of a grater.
- Add tomatoes, onion, cilantro, cucumber, salt, pepper, chile serrano, ketchup and lime juice.
- Mix all ingredients together and taste for flavor.
- Let the mixture sit in the fridge for about 30 minutes.
- Serve on tostadas and add slices of avocado. Enjoy!

Mexican Potatoes

Prep Time: 10 minutes

Cooking Time: 20 minutes

2-3 serving

These potatoes come together ?uickly and have a delicious kick of spice from the serrano peppers.

Ingredients

- 1/3 cup vegetable oil
- 2 medium Idaho potatoes, peeled and diced small
- 1/3 white onion, small dice
- 3 medium serrano peppers, de-seeded and minced
- 1 medium tomato, medium dice
- Salt, to taste

Directions

- Heat the vegetable oil on medium heat in a large frying pan.
- Pan fry the potatoes for about 10-15 minutes, or until golden brown.
- Remove the potatoes and place on paper towels to drain excess oil. Lightly salt potatoes to taste.
- Using the remaining oil in the frying pan, sauté onion and serrano peppers on medium heat, stirring fre?uently.
- Pat diced tomatoes with paper towels to remove excess li?uid.
- Once the onions become translucent, add in the chopped tomato and lightly salt the mixture (about a teaspoon). Stir constantly for about 2-3 minutes.
- Add the fried potatoes back into the pan with the mixture and stir on medium heat for about 2 minutes.
- Serve and enjoy!

Corn Tortillas

Prep Time: 20 minutes

Cooking Time: 15 minutes

Serving: 20- 6 inch tortillas

These corn tortillas, made from scratch with simple ingredients, are a classic staple of traditional Mexican cuisine.

Ingredients

- 2 cups masa harina
- ½ teaspoon salt
- 1½-2 cups hot water

Directions

- In a medium bowl, combine the masa harina and salt.
- Slowly pour the 1 cup of hot water, while mixing with your hands, then pour in a ½ cup and continue mixing. Knead the dough and add more water if needed until a smooth, play-dough like consistency is achieved. The dough should be easily rolled into a ball. If it's sticky, add extra masa harina. If it's crumbly, it needs more water. When the dough is ready, cover the bowl with plastic wrap and let rest for 30 minutes.
- After resting, roll the dough into golf ball-sized balls and cover them with the plastic wrap so they don't dry out.
- Heat a comal or skillet on medium heat.
- Cover a tortilla press with wax paper (or plastic wrap) on both sides and press each ball flat. The tortillas can also be pressed on the countertop with a baking dish or pot instead of a press. Make sure to also use wax paper or plastic wrap to prevent dough from sticking.
- Gently remove the raw tortilla from the press and place on the hot comal. When slight bubbles start to rise, approximately 1 minute, carefully flip the tortilla. Flip again in another 30 seconds-1 minute to check if both sides are lightly browned. Remove from comal when done. Repeat until all tortillas are cooked.
- Stack and wrap them in a clean cloth until time to eat! If you like, you can use a tortilla warmer to keep them warm longer. Enjoy!

Conchas

Prep Time: 90 minutes

Cooking Time: 25-30 minutes

Serving: 6 medium-size conchas

Concha means shell in Spanish. These sweet, fluffy and warm sweet breads are topped with a shell pattern. These are delicious with coffee or hot chocolate.

Ingredients

For the dough

- 2 cups of high-protein flour (bread flour with 4 grams of protein or more per ¼ cup)
- ¼ cup of sugar
- 1 ¼ cup of warm water
- ½ teaspoon of dry baker's yeast
- ¼ teaspoon of salt

For the paste

- ½ cup of high-protein flour (bread flour with 4 grams of protein or more per ¼ cup)
- ½ cup of powdered sugar
- 2 teaspoons (add 3 teaspoons or more, if you want it extra chocolate-y) of cocoa powder, peanut butter or desired flavoring*
- About ¼ cup of coconut oil

Directions

Step 1 For the dough:

- Measure 2 cups of high-protein flour (bread flour with 4 grams of protein or more per ¼ cup) and put them in a mixing bowl.
- Measure 1/4 cup of sugar and add it to your bowl. Mix well with a whisk until the flour and sugar are hard to difference from one another.
- Add 1 ¼ cup of warm water to the mixing bowl. Mix thoroughly until a uniform dough is formed. A silicone spatula works best to mix all the ingredients! Cover your bowl with a damp towel or a plastic bag (to prevent your dough from drying out) and let rest for 30 minutes.
- Step 2

- After the 30 minutes have passed, measure 1/2 of a teaspoon of dry baker's yeast and add it to your dough.
- Measure ¼ teaspoon of salt and add it to your dough.
- Hand-mix your dough. Wet your hand with warm water 2-4 times to prevent dough from sticking to your hand.
- Mix your dough thoroughly until you have mixed well all the ingredients and your dough is elastic and cohesive. Let rest for one to two hours or until dough has doubled in size.

For the paste:

- In a clean mixing bowl, add ½ cup of high-protein flour (bread flour with 4 grams of protein or more per ¼ cup) and ½ cup of powdered sugar. At this point, you can add the flavor for your concha paste. For example, if it is a chocolate concha, add 2 teaspoons (add 3 teaspoons or more if you want it extra chocolate-y) of cocoa powder to your bowl. Mix well with a whisk.
- Melt ¼ of cup of coconut oil and add it to your bowl. Mix well using a silicone spatula (recommended.)
- With your hands, form the paste into a ball. Cut in 6 eual pieces.

To make your conchas:

- Find a clean surface to work. Any countertop can be used as your workstation.
- Grab a handful of flour and dust your countertop. This is done to prevent your dough from sticking to the surface.
- On the flour dusted area, pour your dough that has been resting and should have risen to double its size

by now. If it has not risen to double in size, let it rest until it has done so and then proceed with this step.

- With a kitchen knife, cut your dough into 6 or more pieces. Shape into little balls and cover them with a little bit of melted coconut oil. Put on a clean baking tray and let them rest for 30 minutes or so while you work on your paste.
- Using a plastic bag cut in half, put each pre-cut ball of paste in the middle of it and press with a cutting board or something flat but heavy to make a tortilla-like paste. As you are working on each ball of paste to make your topping for your conchas, start putting them on top of your balls of dough as you work through them. Keep going until each dough ball has its own topping.
- Score your conchas to any design desired. Make them uni▢ue!
- Put your conchas in the oven for 30 minutes or until golden brown at 350 F.
- Take out from the oven using a heat-resistant glove and let them cool a little bit.
- Enjoy your freshly baked conchas with your friends and family with a cup of vegan hot cocoa or coffee.
- Enjoy!

Fruit Cup

Prep Time: 10-15 minutes

Cook Time: 0 minutes

Serving 6 cups

In Mexico, fruit is often enjoyed with a generous coating of salt, lime juice and chili powder. This recipe can be easily adapted to include all kids of fruit.

Ingredients

- 6 cups of various fruits, diced in 1-inch chunks
- Recommended fruits: apple, pineapple, cucumber, strawberry, grapes, cherry, mango, coconut, kiwi
- 1/2 cup of lime juice
- 2 tablespoons of chili powder
- 2 tablespoons of salt

Directions

- Mix the chili and salt.
- Add diced fruit in a large bowl.
- Pour lime juice over the fruit and toss to coat.
- Sprinkle chili/salt mixture over the fruit.
- If possible, chill the bowl of fruit in refrigerator for at least an hour before serving

Green Chile Salsa

Prep Time: 10-15 minutes

Cooking Time: 40 minutes

Serves: 2

This Green Chile Salsa recipe gets its kick from Anaheim peppers and jalapeños. It's the perfect appetizer with chips or drizzled over your favorite Mexican dishes.

Ingredients

- 10 tomatillos, outer husk removed
- 5 Anaheim peppers
- 3 jalapeño peppers
- 1 large onion, sliced
- 1 whole garlic bulb
- ½ cup water
- 1 – 2 teaspoons salt
- Juice of 1 small lime
- Cilantro (optional)

Directions

- Heat oven to 425 F.
- Remove the husk and slice tomatillos in half.
- Slice a small portion of the top of the garlic bulb off. This will allow you to remove the cloves more easily after the garlic is roasted. Wrap garlic bulb in foil.
- Cover a shallow baking tray with parchment paper. Place the sliced tomatillos, Anaheim peppers, jalapeños, sliced onions, and wrapped garlic bulb on the baking sheet, and place in the oven to roast.
- Watch carefully so your peppers, onions, and tomatillos char, but do not burn. After about 20 minutes, the skins of the chiles should begin to char. You want them to be well-roasted; the char adds a rich flavor. Turn them over to char on the other side. Total time may be 30 to 40 minutes depending on your oven and the size of the ingredients.
- When the other side is roasted, remove from the oven. Sweat the peppers by placing them in a tightly sealed container. This will help loosen the skin of the peppers and easily remove them. Keep them in the container for about 10 – 15 minutes to cool.
- After the peppers have cooled, remove the skins. Use gloves for this process so that your hands do not burn

from the hot peppers. It is okay to leave a little bit of char if you can't remove it, but too much will not taste good.

- For salsa that is not too spicy, remove the stem and seeds. If you love hot salsa, remove stems only.
- Unwrap the garlic from the foil. From the bottom of the bulb, squeeze out the roasted cloves towards the top of the bulb where you sliced the top off. The garlic should be soft enough to slide right out.
- Add garlic, onions, tomatillos, peppers, salt, water, and lime to your food processor. Begin with 1 teaspoon of salt—add more to taste if necessary.
- Blend the ingredients in the food processor until there is an even and consistent texture. Do not over blend. If salsa is too thick, add more water.
- Taste and adjust flavors as needed.
- If using cilantro, add it to the mixture and pulse only 3 or 4 times. Over processing the cilantro will cause it to become more bitter. Enjoy!

Guacamole

Prep Time: 5 minutes

Cooking Time: 0 minutes

Serves: 2

Guacamole is a citrusy and creamy addition to any meal, and it's delicious on its own. Enjoy with chips or as a side to your entree.

Ingredients

- 4 avocados
- 2 medium tomatoes, diced
- ½ yellow onion, diced
- 3 tablespoons cilantro, chopped
- 1 lime, juiced
- ½ teaspoon salt
- ½ teaspoon fresh black peppe

Directions

- Slice the avocados in half, remove the pit and skin and place in a bowl.
- Mash the avocado with a fork and add the squeezed lime.
- Add the diced tomatoes, onions, and cilantro.
- Season with salt and pepper 5 Serve and enjoy

Pineapple Empanadas

Prep Time: 20 minutes

Cooking Time: 30 minutes

Serves: 12 empanadas

A perfect dessert. These sweet empanadas are filled with pineapple preserves. Enjoy these warm, flaky hand pies with coffee!

Ingredients

For Dough

- 2 cups unbleached white flour
- 2 tablespoons evaporated cane sweetener
- 2 teaspoons sea salt
- 2 teaspoons baking powder
- ⅓ cup vegetable shortening
- ½ cup water
- 1 batch filling, pineapple or pumpkin
- Agave nectar for assembly

For Pineapple Filling

- 1 (8-ounce) jar pineapple preserves
- For Pumpkin Filling Option

Pumpkin Filling recipe

- 1 (15-ounce) can pumpkin
- ¾ cup brown sugar
- 4 tablespoons cornstarch
- 1 teaspoon cinnamon
- 1 tablespoon molasses
- 1 teaspoon vanilla

Directions

For the Dough

- In a large bowl, mix together flour, sweetener, salt, and baking powder.
- Add vegetable shortening to dry ingredients and use fingers to mix thoroughly until mixture resembles coarse crumbs.
- Add water and knead together.
- Cover dough and place in refrigerator for 5-10 minutes.

For the Pumpkin Filling Option

- In a medium size bowl, mix all ingredients until incorporated.
- Taste and adjust as needed. It shouldn't be too wet to scoop into the center of the dough circles.

For the Empanadas

- Preheat oven to 350 degrees.
- Line a baking sheet with parchment paper or non-stick silicone baking mat and set aside.
- On a large, floured surface, roll out the dough and cut circles about 3½ inches in diameter (roughly 12 circles).
- Place a small spoonful of pineapple preserves (or pumpkin filling) in the center of each circle and lightly dab the edges with agave nectar.
- Fold the dough over to enclose the filling and seal the edges together by pressing down with a fork.
- Place the empanadas on the baking sheet and bake for 15 minutes.
- Remove sheet from oven and glaze empanadas with agave nectar.
- Set sheet back in oven and broil empanadas until they are golden brown. Approximately 3 minutes.

Chapter 4: Plant-Based Lunch & Dinner Recipes

White Pizza

Delicious white pizza with Arugula and Red Onion!

Serves 2

Total Time: 30 min

Ingredients

- 1 can cannellini beans
- 2 cloves garlic
- 1/3 cup nutritional yeast
- 1 lemon
- 3/4 teaspoon dried basil
- 1/2 teaspoon dried oregano
- 1 red onion
- 1 cup arugula
- 1 package organic pizza dough
- 1/2 cup whole wheat flour
- 1 tablespoon oilve oil
- salt and pepper to taste

Instructions

- Preheat your oven to 450°F. Punch the dough down to knead and flatten it. On a lightly floured work surface, roll out or stretch the dough into a circle of 1/4-inch thickness.
- Place the dough onto a pizza pan or baking sheet lightly oiled with olive oil. Stretch dough further into a circle or oval. Bake on the bottom rack of the oven for 8 minutes.
- While the crust bakes, drain and rinse the beans. Cut the lemon in half and juice into a small bowl, picking out any seeds. Mince the garlic. In a food processor or blender, combine the beans, garlic, nutritional yeast, lemon juice, basil and oregano. Season with salt and pepper. Blend until mixture is smooth and consistent. If the mixture is too thick, add a tablespoon or two of water and pulse.
- Remove the crust from the oven and spread the blended bean mixture to within a half-inch of the edge of the crust. Put back in the oven and bake until the crust is nicely browned, about 10-12 minutes.

- While the pizza is baking, heat 1 tablespoon of olive oil in a medium-sized skillet over medium heat. Thinly slice the onion and sauté until softened, about 4 minutes. Add the arugula and sauté until wilted, 2-3 minutes longer. Season with salt and pepper. When the pizza comes out of the oven, top with the sautéed onion and arugula. Cut into fourths, serve immediately, and enjoy!

Linguine Recipe

Serves 2

Total Time 40 min

Ingredients

- 3 shallots
- 2 large garlic cloves, peeled
- 1 package Fieldroast vegan sausages
- 1 cup almond milk
- 1 28-ounce can diced tomatoes

- 1 tablespoon dried sage
- 1/2 teaspoon crushed red pepper flakes
- 1 pound linguine
- 2 tablespoons olive oil

Instructions

- Bring a large pot of water to a boil over medium-high heat. Peel and chop the shallots. Mince the garlic. Roughly chop the sausages. Set aside. While the water is heating, warm 2 tablespoons of olive oil in a large skillet. Add garlic and chopped shallots and saute over medium-high heat for about 3 minutes.
- Heat 2 tablespoons of olive oil in skillet over medium heat. Sauté garlic and shallots until soft, about 3 minutes. Add sausage and cook for 5 minutes. Turn to low heat and add almond milk and simmer for 5 minutes. Add tomatoes, sage and crushed red pepper flakes (use as much or as little depending on your affinity for heat). Simmer until sauce thickens, about 15 minutes. Stir occasionally.
- When water is boiling, add linguini and cook until soft, about 5 minutes. Drain pasta while saving 1/2 cup of pasta water for sauce.
- Once sauce has thickened, add linguini to sauce over low heat. Combine well making sure pasta is fully coated. If necessary, add reserved pasta water to fully coat. Serve and enjoy!

Bowtie Pasta With Mushrooms

Serves 2

Total Time : 30 Min

Ingredients

- 1/4 cup + 1 tablespoon olive oil
- 1/2 teaspoon ground pepper
- 1 tablespoon + 1/2 teaspoon salt
- 2 tablespoons parsley

- 2 tablespoons freshly squeezed lemon juice
- 1/4 cup flax oil
- 1/2 cup Marsala wine
- 1 vegetable bouillon cube
- 2 pounds mushrooms
- 1/2 cup shallots
- 1 pound bowtie pasta

Instructions

- Rinse and dry all produce. Fill a large pot with water and add a tablespoon of olive oil and a pinch of salt. Bring to a boil, and add the pasta, stirring well to prevent sticking. Cook for about 12 minutes, or done to your liking. Strain and set aside.
- While the pasta is cooking, peel and chop shallot. Chop parsley and mushrooms. Cut lemon in half and squeeze juice into small bowl. Set aside.
- Heat ¼ cup olive oil in large sauté pan over medium heat. Add the shallots, cook and stir for about 2 minutes until softened and lightly colored. Add the mushrooms and stir well. Cover the pan until the mushrooms for about 1 minute until the mushrooms release their liquid.
- Remove the lid, add bouillon cube, a pinch of salt and pepper. Stir well, and cook for 5 more minutes, or until the liquid is absorbed and the mushrooms begin to brown. Add the Marsala wine stirring to incorporate any browned bits into the sauce.
- Toss the pasta into the pan with mushroom mixture. Remove from heat and add the flax oil, lemon juice and parsley, and toss well. Serve immediately.

Penne Pasta, Garlic & Olive oil Recipe

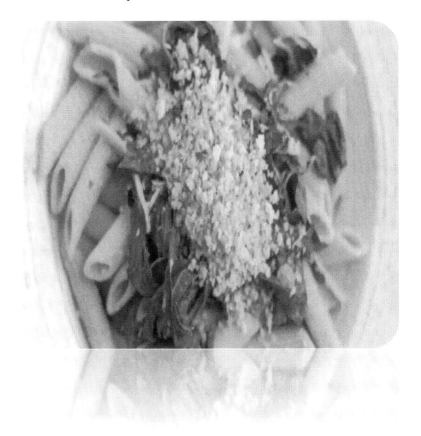

Serves 2

Total Time: 30 min

Ingredients

- 16 oz. whole grain penne pasta
- 2 tablespoons olive oil
- 4 garlic cloves, peeled
- 1/2 cup panko bread crumbs
- 1 tablespoon nutritional yeast
- 1 teaspoon red pepper flakes

- 1 bunch collard greens
- 1 lemon
- spice pack

Instructions

- Prep: Rinse and dry the produce. Zest lemon into a small bowl, cut lemon in half and juice into another small bowl. Mince the garlic. Remove the stems from the collard greens and stack the leaves. Tightly roll the leaves and thinly slice into 1/2 inch ribbons.
- Bring a large pot of salted water to a boil. Add the whole wheat pasta and cook until al dente, about 10-12 minutes.
- Place the minced garlic on a cutting board and using the flat part of your knife, run over the garlic until a paste is formed.
- Add the garlic and spice pack of nutritional yeast, panko bread crumbs and red pepper flakes in a small pan over medium-low heat and stir constantly until the bread crumbs get golden brown, and you smell a nutty aroma, about 1-2 minutes. Turn off heat and set aside.
- Heat 2 tablespoons olive oil in a medium sauté pan over medium heat. Add the collard greens and cook until collards are wilted and cooked through, about 5 minutes. Add in the pasta and stir.
- To serve, top the pasta and collards with the bread crumb mixture, lemon juice and lemon zest. Eat immediately and enjoy!

Brown Rice Pesto Bowls Lunch Recipe

Serves 2

Total Time: 5 min

Ingredients

- 2 packages precooked brown rice
- 7 oz artichoke hearts
- ¼ cup Kalamata olives
- ¼ cup vegan basil pesto
- 2 tbsp Soy-Free Vegan Parmesan

Instructions

- Make a 2 inch tear in the top of the brown rice bag and microwave for 1 minute. Drain the artichoke hearts. Check the Kalamata olives for pits and remove if present.
- Divide the cooked brown rice into 2 servings and stir in basil pesto. Top with artichoke hearts, olives and parmesan.

Pesto Pasta, Pine Nuts & Carrot Noodle Recipe

Prep Time:4 minutes

Cook Time: 6 minutes

Serves 1

Ingredients

- 1 package Green Giant Veggie Spirals
- 3 Tablespoons prepared pesto
- 1/4 Cup pine nuts
- 1/4 Cup basil

- 1 Tablespoon lemon juice
- 1 Tablespoon honey

Instructions

- Prepare the carrot Veggie Spirals either in the microwave or in a skillet according to the package directions. You can use the microwave cooking method for a little bit ⍰uicker results.
- While the carrots are cooking, roughly chop the pine nuts and thinly slice the basil. Mix the chopped pine nuts and basil together with the lemon juice and honey. Set aside.
- Gently toss the drained carrot Veggie Spirals with the pesto sauce. Top the Carrot Pesto Pasta with the pine nut mixture and enjoy!

Pasta & Beetballs

Delicious recipe made with Broccoli & Rosemary Lemon Butter!

Serves 2

Total Time: 35 min

Ingredients

- ¼ oz fresh rosemary
- 1 shallot
- 2 cloves garlic
- 1 lemon
- 3 tbsp gluten-free rolled oats

- 4 oz shredded red beets
- ¼ cup green peas
- 1 tbsp flaxseed meal
- ¼ cup macadamia nuts
- 8 oz Banza rotini
- 3 tbsp vegan butter
- 6 oz broccoli florets
- 1 tbsp olive oil
- Salt and pepper

Instructions

- Preheat oven to 400°F. Place a large pot of salted water on to boil. Mince 1 tbsp of the rosemary leaves. Peel and mince the shallot. Peel and mince the garlic. Zest and halve the lemon.
- Add the rolled oats to a food processor and pulse until coarsely ground. Add just the lemon zest, just half the garlic, shredded beets, green peas, flaxseed meal, macadamia nuts, ½ tsp salt, and a pinch of pepper. Blend well to combine. Form into 6 beetballs and place on a baking sheet. Drizzle with 1 tbsp olive oil and roll to coat. Roast until firm, about 20 to 23 minutes.
- Add the rotini to the boiling water, stir, and cook until al dente, about 8 to 10 minutes. Reserve ½ cup of the pasta water and then drain the rotini.
- Place a large skillet over medium-high heat with the butter. Once the butter is hot, add the minced rosemary, minced shallot, remaining garlic, and a pinch of salt, and cook until softened, about 2 to 3 minutes. Add the pasta water and lemon juice, reduce heat to low. Cook until thickened, taste, and adjust seasoning with salt and pepper.
- Add 1 inch of salted water to the large pot and return to a boil. Once boiling, add the broccoli and cook until

crisp-tender, about 1 to 2 minutes and then drain. Return the Banza pasta to the large skillet along with the rosemary lemon butter, toss well to combine. Taste and season with salt and pepper.

- Divide the pasta with rosemary lemon butter and between large plates and top with beetballs. Serve with broccoli and garnish with any remaining rosemary sprigs.

Thai Peanut Chickpea Bowls With Cucumber

Serves 2

Total Time: 5 min

Ingredients

- 8 oz precooked brown rice
- 13.4 oz chickpeas
- 1 cucumber
- ¼ oz fresh cilantro
- ¼ cup peanut sauce
- ¼ cup peanuts

Instructions

- Make a 2" tear on the top of the brown rice bag, and microwave for 1 minute. Thinly slice the cucumber. Pick the cilantro leaves from the stems. Drain, rinse, and dry the chickpeas.
- Mix the spicy peanut sauce with 2 tsp water. Divide the brown rice into 2 servings. Top with chickpeas, sliced cucumbers, and peanuts. Drizzle with spicy peanut sauce and sprinkle with cilantro leaves.

Flatbread Recipe

Awesome and delicious recipe with Sweet Corn Puree and Balsamic Glaze .

Serves 2

Total Time: 30 min

Ingrdients

- 1 clove garlic
- 1 shallot
- 2 summer squash
- 1 ear fresh corn

- ½ oz fresh parsley
- 4 oz roasted red peppers
- 2 tbsp vegan sour cream
- ¼ cup balsamic vinegar
- 1 tbsp turbinado sugar
- 2 multigrain flatbreads
- 3 tbsp vegan parmesan
- 1 tbsp + 1 tsp olive oil
- Salt and pepper

Instructions

- Peel and slice the garlic. Peel and thinly slice the shallot. Use a peeler to shave the summer squash into thin ribbons. Cut the corn kernels off the cob. Pick the parsley leaves from the stems. Drain the roasted red peppers. Add the parsley leaves and roasted red peppers to a small bowl.
- Place a large nonstick skillet over medium heat with 1 tbsp olive oil. Once the oil is hot, add the sliced garlic and sliced shallot and cook until softened, about 2 to 3 minutes. Add the corn kernels and a pinch of salt and pepper and cook until charred in places, about 3 to 4 minutes.
- Reserve ¼ cup of the corn mixture for garnish. Transfer the remaining corn mixture to a blender or food processor with ¼ tsp salt and the sour cream. Blend, adding water, 1 tbsp at a time, until smooth. Taste, and adjust seasoning with salt and pepper.
- Place a small saucepan over high heat with the balsamic vinegar and sugar. Bring to a boil and cook until the sugar dissolves and the sauce coats the back of a spoon, about 1 to 2 minutes (watch carefully, this happens quickly). Transfer to a small bowl to cool.
- Set the oven to broil on low. Place flatbreads in the oven, directly on the rack. Bake until slightly crisp,

about 3 to 5 minutes. In a large bowl, toss the shaved squash, 1 tsp olive oil, and a pinch of salt and pepper. Spread half of the sweet corn purée on each toasted flatbread and sprinkle the reserved corn on top. Layer on the summer squash ribbons and top with parmesan.

- Place flatbreads on a baking sheet and broil until lightly browned on top, about 4 to 6 minutes.
- Drizzle the summer squash flatbreads with balsamic glaze and top with parsley and roasted red peppers.

Garlic Roasted Broccoli With Zucchini Noodles & Tofu

Serves 2

Total Time: 35 min

Ingredients

- 6 cloves garlic
- 1 shallot
- 2 zucchini
- 15.5 oz Wildwood Organic Extra Firm Sprouted Tofu
- 1 lemon
- 2 tbsp capers

- 2 tbsp white balsamic vinegar
- 2 tsp vegetable broth concentrate
- 6 oz broccoli florets
- 2 tbsp vegan butter
- ¼ oz fresh basil
- 2 tbsp + 1 tsp olive oil
- Salt and pepper

Instructions

- Preheat the oven to 400°F. Peel and smash the garlic with the side of the knife. Peel and mince the shallot. Trim the zucchini and slice lengthwise into ¼ inch thick planks. Stack and cut the planks into thin strips to make zucchini noodles or zoodles. Drain the tofu, pay dry with paper towels, and cut into 1 inch cubes. Halve the lemon.
- Place a large nonstick skillet over medium-high heat with 1 tbsp olive oil. Once hot, add the cubed tofu and cook, tossing frequently, until crispy on all sides, about 3 to 5 minutes. Sprinkle with salt and transfer to a paper-towel-lined plate. Add another 1 tbsp olive oil to the skillet along with the smashed garlic and minced shallot. Reduce heat to low and cook until lightly browned, about 1 minute.
- Add the capers, white balsamic vinegar, and juice from the lemon. Sprinkle with salt and pepper, then add the vegetable broth concentrate and ½ cup water. Bring to a boil and reduce heat to a simmer. Cook the sauce until thickened, about 2 to 4 minutes.
- Add the broccoli florets to a baking sheet and toss with 1 tsp olive oil and a pinch of salt and pepper. Roast broccoli in the oven until browned and crisp in places, about 6 to 8 minutes.
- Add the zoodles to the skillet and cook until bright green and just tender, about 2 to 3 minutes. Stir in the

crispy tofu and butter and season tofu piccata with salt.
- Hand-tear the basil leaves. Divide the tofu piccata between large bowls and top with torn basil. Serve with roasted broccoli.

Black Bean Burrito

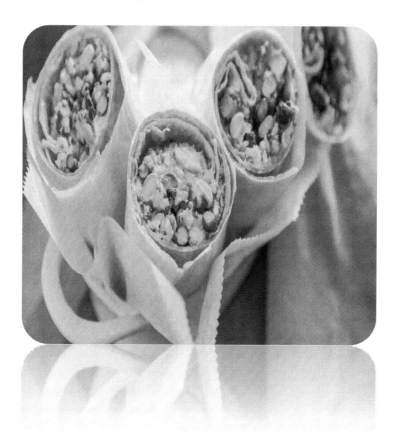

serves: 2

Prep & Cook Time: 5 min

Ingredients

- 8 oz precooked rice and vegetable quinoa blend
- 13.4 oz black beans
- 1 avocado
- 2 whole wheat tortillas
- ¼ cup pickled jalapeños

- 2 tbsp Soy-Free Vegenaise
- 2 tbsp hot sauce

Instructions

For the burritos

- Make a small 2 inch tear in the top of the brown rice bag and microwave for 1 minute. Drain, rinse, and dry the black beans. Halve the avocado, remove the pit, scoop out the flesh, and slice.

Serving

- In a small bowl, combine the Vegenaise and hot sauce. Spread the spicy mayo onto the tortillas. Top with rice, black beans, sliced avocado, and pickled jalapeños. Fold the sides in and wrap tightly.

Black Bean Bowls

Delicious lunch recipe with avocado and lime dressing!

Servings: 2

Prep & Cook Time: 5 min

Ingredients

- 1 package precooked brown rice
- 1 package black beans
- 1 avocado
- 1 lime
- ⅓ cup High Omega Vegan Ranch

- 2 tsp taco seasoning

Instructions

For the bowls

- Add the brown rice to a small bowl and microwave for 1 minute. Drain, rinse, and dry the black beans. Halve, deseed, and dice the avocado flesh. Halve the lime. Combine the ranch dressing, taco seasoning, and lime juice in a small bowl.

Serving

- Divide the brown rice and black beans between bowls. Top with avocado.
- Dress with ranch lime dressing. Enjoy!

Plantain Bowl

A Perfect lunch recipe loaded with Guacamole and Black Beans.

Serves: 2

Prep & Cook Time:5 min

Ingredients

- 6 oz Lacinato kale
- 1 can black beans
- 1 plantain
- 1 lime

- 1 red onion
- Fresh cilantro
- 1 avocado
- ¼ cup pumpkin seeds
- ¼ cup dried cranberries
- 1 tbsp + 1 tsp vegetable oil
- Salt and pepper

Instructions

For the Vegetables

- Destem the kale and roughly chop the leaves. Drain and rinse the black beans. Peel the plantain and cut into ½ inch thick slices. Halve the lime.

For the guacamole

- Peel and dice the red onion. Roughly chop the cilantro. Halve the avocado, scoop the flesh into a medium bowl and mash with a fork. Add the juice from the lime, as much of the red onion as you'd like, chopped cilantro, and a pinch of salt. Mix well, mashing together with a fork, to make a chunky guacamole. Fold in the pumpkin seeds and dried cranberries.

Fry the plantain

- Place a large nonstick skillet over medium-high heat with 1 tbsp vegetable oil. Once the oil is hot, add the sliced plantain and cook until lightly browned about 3 to 4 minutes per side. Transfer the crispy plantains to a plate and cover to keep warm.
- Sauté the kale and beans
- Return the skillet to medium-high heat with 1 tsp vegetable oil. Add the chopped kale and a pinch of salt and pepper. Cook until the kale is bright green and

wilted, about 1 to 2 minutes. Add the black beans and reduce the heat to low. Cook until hot, about 3 to 5 minutes.

Serving

- Divide the black beans and kale between large bowls. Top with crispy plantains and loaded guacamole

Mezze Salad

Delicous mezze salad with marinated chickpeas & tart cherries.

Servings 2

Prep & Cook Time: 5 min

Ingredients

- 4 oz Arcadian greens
- 6 oz shredded carrot
- 2 tbsp red wine vinegar
- 6 oz marinated chickpeas
- ¼ cup dried tart cherries
- 4 brown rice stuffed grape leaves

- 2 oz hummus

Instructions

- Add the Arcadian greens and shredded carrots to a large bowl and toss with red wine vinegar and a pinch of salt and pepper.
- Divide the dressed salads into 2 servings. Top with marinated chickpeas, dried cherries, stuffed grape leaves, and hummus.

Chickpea Lettuce Cups With Walnuts

Serves: 2

Prep & Cook Time :5 min

Ingredients

- 1 shallot
- 13.4 oz chickpeas
- ¼ cup Follow Your Heart Soy Free Vegenaise
- ¼ cup walnuts
- 1 oz dried cranberries
- 2 heads Roma crunch lettuce

Instructions

- Peel and mince the shallot. Drain, rinse, and dry the chickpeas. Add the chickpeas to a large bowl and mash with the back of a fork. Add the Vegenaise and a good pinch of salt and pepper. Stir to combine. Fold in the minced shallot, walnuts, and dried cranberries.
- To serve, scoop the chickpea salad into the Roma crunch leaves.

Kale Beet Salad With Dried Cranberries

Serves: 2

Prep & Cook Time : 5 min

Ingredients

- 1 cucumber
- 8 oz kale beet blend
- 13.4 oz chickpeas
- 2 tbsp red wine vinegar
- Salt and pepper
- 1 tbsp olive oil
- 2 oz dried cranberries

- ¼ cup walnuts
- 2 oz Treeline scallion cashew cheese

Instructions

- Drain and rinse the chickpeas. Thinly slice the cucumber. Add the kale beet blend and chickpeas to a large bowl and toss with the red wine vinegar, 1 tbsp olive oil, and a pinch of salt and pepper.
- Divide the dressed salads between bowls. Top with sliced cucumber, dried cranberries and walnuts. Finish with scallion cashew cheese.

Burrito Bowls

Simple recipe with brown rice and guacamole.

Serves 2

Prep & Cook Time : 5 Min

Ingredients

- 8.8 oz precooked brown rice
- 13.4 oz black beans
- ½ oz fresh cilantro
- 1 lime
- ½ cup corn kernels

- 4 oz guacamole
- 2 tsp sriracha packets

Instructions

- Make a 2 inch tear in the top of the brown rice bag and microwave for 1 minute. Drain and rinse the black beans. Roughly chop the cilantro leaves and stems. Divide the brown rice into 2 servings. Top with the black beans, chopped cilantro, corn kernels, and guacamole. When you're ready to eat, halve the lime and squeeze the lime juice over the bowls.
- Top with as much of the sriracha as you'd like.

Mexican Fiesta Recipe

Serves 2

Prep & Cook Time : 30 min

Ingredients

- 2 garlic cloves, peeled
- 1 tablespoon olive oil
- 1 serrano pepper
- 1 cup quinoa
- 1 cub vegetable broth
- 1 can black beans
- 1 can diced tomatoes

- 1 can corn kernels
- 1 teaspoon chili powder
- 1/2 teaspoon cumin
- 1 avocado
- 1 lime
- 2 tablespoons cilantro
- salt and pepper, to taste

Instructions

- Prep: Rinse and dry the produce. Mince the garlic. Slice the Serrano pepper in half lengthwise, discard the seeds and stem and mince into small pieces.
- If you want a less spicy dish, use less of the pepper. Drain and rinse the black beans and corn.
- Slice the avocado in half lengthwise, remove and discard pit, slice avocado into 1/4 inch cubes.
- Slice the lime in half and juice into a small bowl, set aside. Remove the cilantro leaves from stems and roughly chop.
- Heat 1 tablespoon olive oil in a large skillet over medium high heat. Add garlic and serrano pepper and cook until fragrant, about 1 minute.
- Stir in ⬚uinoa and toast, stirring constantly for 1 minute.
- Add the vegetable broth, black beans, tomatoes, corn, chili powder and cumin. Stir to incorporate.
- Bring the mixture to a boil, cover and reduce heat to low and simmer until ⬚uinoa is cooked through, about 20 minutes.
- Add avocado, lime juice and cilantro and stir to incorporate.
- Serve immediately, enjoy!

Beluga Lentil Tacos Recipe

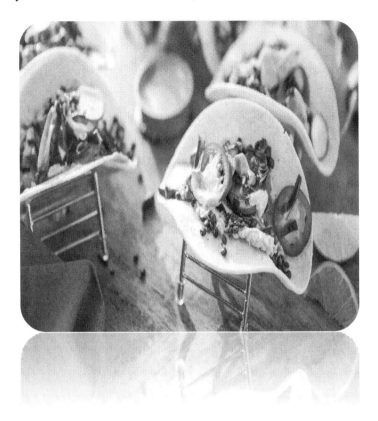

Serving 2

Total Time: 30 min

Ingredients

- ⅓ cup beluga lentils
- 1 tsp cumin
- 1 packet vegetable broth concentrate
- 2 radish
- 1 jalapeño
- 1 lime
- Pea shoots

- 1 avocado
- 3 tbsp Follow Your Heart Vegenaise
- ½ tsp chipotle paste
- 6 corn tortillas
- Salt

Instructions

- Preheat oven to 350°F. Combine the beluga lentils, cumin, vegetable broth concentrate, and ⅔ cup water in a small saucepan. Bring to a boil, cover, and reduce heat to low. Simmer until the lentils are tender and the water is absorbed, about 20 to 25 minutes.
- Thinly slice the radish. Thinly slice the jalapeño.
- Halve the avocado and remove the pit. Scoop the flesh from the skin, and add to a medium bowl. Add the juice from half the the lime, and a pinch of salt and pepper. Mash the ⬚uick guacamole well with fork.
- In a small bowl, combine the Vegenaise, 1 tsp water, and as much of the chipotle paste as you'd like. Mix the chipotle crema well and season with salt.
- Wrap the corn tortillas in foil or a dish towel and warm them in the oven, about 5 minutes. In a medium bowl, combine the pea shoots, sliced radish, and as much of the jalapeño as you'd like. Add the juice from the remaining lime half and a pinch of salt. Gently toss the pea shoot slaw to combine.
- To build your tacos, divide the quick guacamole between the tortillas and spread it out a bit. Top each with about 2 tbsp of the beluga lentils (the guac will help them stick!), then layer on the pea shoot slaw. Drizzle with chipotle crema.

Crunch Wraps Recipe With Black Beans

Serves 2

Prep & Cook Time: 35 min

Ingredients

- 1 onion
- 4 oz shredded green cabbage
- 1 tsp Mexican oregano
- 1 tsp turbinado sugar

- 2 tbsp apple cider vinegar
- 2 garlic cloves
- 1 poblano pepper
- 1 Roma tomato
- 13.4 oz black beans
- 6 oz tomatillos
- 2 tbsp vegan sour cream
- 2 gluten-free wraps
- ¼ cup vegan mozzarella
- 2 tbsp + 1 tsp olive oil

Instructions

For the curtido

- Peel and thinly slice the onion. Add just half of the sliced onion to a large bowl along with the cabbage, oregano, sugar, apple cider vinegar, and a pinch of salt and pepper. Mix curtido with your hands for a minute to break down the cabbage slightly.
- Peel the garlic. Trim, deseed, and thinly slice the poblano. Slice the tomato. Drain and rinse the black beans. Peel the papery husks off the tomatillos, then rinse and dice them.

For the tomatillo sauce

- Place a small saucepan over medium-high heat. Add the garlic, diced tomatillos, ½ cup water, 1 tbsp olive oil, ¼ tsp salt, and bring to a simmer. Cook, stirring occasionally, until tomatillos are softened and the liquid thickens slightly, about 5 to 6 minutes. Add the cooked tomatillos to a blender and blend until smooth. Add the sour cream, blend again, taste, and adjust seasoning with salt and pepper.
- Place a large nonstick skillet over medium-high heat with 1 tbsp olive oil. Once hot, add the remaining

101

sliced onion, sliced poblano, and a pinch of salt. Cook until softened, about 3 to 4 minutes. Add the beans, and cook until hot, about 2 to 3 minutes. Mash some of the beans with the back of a fork.

- Lay the tortillas on a clean work surface and sprinkle each with shredded mozzarella. Top with sliced tomato, black beans, and a small amount of curtido. Wrap by gently folding in the sides one at a time. Rinse and dry the skillet and return to medium heat with 1 tsp olive oil and the crunch wraps, seam side down. Cook until sealed and crisp, about 1 minute per side.

- Divide the black bean crunch wraps and between large plates with the remaining curtido on the side. Drizzle with tomatillo sour cream. Enjoy!

Mexican Molletes Pico de Gallo Recipe

Servings: 2

Total Time: 35 min

Ingredients

- 2 torta rolls
- 2 radishes
- 1 Roma tomato
- 1 lime
- 1 red onion
- 1 head Roma crunch lettuce
- 1 chipotle pepper in adobo

- 1 jalapeño
- 13.4 oz pinto beans
- ½ cup vegan shredded mozzarella
- ¼ cup Follow Your Heart High Omega Vegan Ranch
- 3 tbsp olive oil
- Salt and pepper

Instructions

- Preheat the oven to 400°F. Slice the torta rolls in half. Thinly slice the radishes into matchsticks. Dice the tomato. Halve the lime. Peel and finely dice the red onion. Roughly chop the lettuce. Mince the chipotle pepper. Thinly slice the jalapeño into rounds. Drain and rinse the pinto beans.
- In a medium bowl, combine the sliced radishes, diced tomato, half the lime juice, just ¼ cup diced onion, and a pinch of salt. Mix radish pico de gallo well to combine.
- Place a small saucepan over medium heat with 2 tsp vegetable oil. Add the remaining diced onion and cook until softened, about 3 to 5 minutes. Add the pinto beans and smash half with the back of a fork. Add 2 tbsp water and as much minced chipotle pepper as you'd like. Cook until the beans are hot, about 2 to 3 minutes. Add the remaining lime juice and a pinch of salt, off of the heat.
- Place the halved torta rolls on a baking sheet, cut side up, and drizzle each with 1 tsp olive oil. Sprinkle with a pinch of salt and pepper and toast until golden brown, about 3 to 4 minutes. Flip the bread and toast for an additional 3 to 4 minutes. Remove the baking sheet from the oven and flip the toasted torta halves cut side up again.
- Divide the refried beans between the toasted torta rolls and top with shredded mozzarella. Toast in the

oven until the cheese melts and begins to brown, about 2 to 3 minutes. Divide the Mexican molletes between large plates and top each with 1 tbsp radish pico de gallo.

- In a large bowl, combine the chopped lettuce, 1 tbsp olive oil, a pinch of salt and pepper, and any remaining radish pico de gallo. Toss the salad well, then divide between the plates with the molletes. Drizzle everything with ranch dressing and top with sliced jalapeño.
- Enjoy!

Summer Squash Tacos

Make this recipe with Tomatillo Salsa and Charred Corn.

Serves 2

Prep & Cook Time: 35 min

Ingredients

- 1 onion
- 2 garlic cloves
- ¼ oz fresh cilantro
- 4 oz tomatillos
- 1 jalapeño

- 1 ear sweet corn
- 1 yellow squash
- 1 lime
- 6 corn tortillas
- 2 tbsp vegan sour cream
- 2 oz shredded red cabbage
- 2 tbsp vegetable oil
- Salt and pepper

Instructions

- Peel and finely dice the onion. Add just ¼ cup diced onion to a medium bowl. Peel and mince the garlic. Finely chop the cilantro leaves and stems. Remove the husk from the tomatillos, rinse, and dice the flesh. Trim, deseed, and mince the jalapeño. Cut the corn kernels off the cob. Trim and slice the summer squash into half moons. Halve the lime.
- Add just half the minced garlic, chopped cilantro, diced tomatillo, as much minced jalapeño as you'd like, just half the lime juice, and a pinch of salt to the bowl with the diced onion. Stir tomatillo salsa to combine.
- Place a large nonstick skillet over medium-high heat. Once hot, add the corn kernels and cook until blackened in spots, about 3 to 5 minutes. Transfer to a medium bowl.
- Return the skillet to medium-high heat with 1 tbsp vegetable oil. Once the oil is hot, add the remaining diced onion, remaining minced garlic, cut summer squash, and a pinch of salt and pepper. Cook until charred on both sides, about 8 to 10 minutes, and season with salt and pepper. Transfer the cooked squash to the bowl with the charred corn.
- Wipe the skillet clean and return to medium-high heat with 1 tbsp vegetable oil. Add 3 corn tortillas in a

single layer. Top each tortilla with the squash and corn mixture, then fold in half. Cook until crispy, about 1 minute per side. Transfer the summer squash tacos to a plate, then repeat with the remaining tortillas.

- In a small bowl, combine the remaining lime juice, sour cream, and a pinch of salt. Stir the lime crema. Top the summer squash tacos with tomatillo salsa, shredded red cabbage, and lime crema. Enjoy!

Smoky Portobello Tacos With Spanish Rice

Serves 2

Prep and Cook Time: 30 min

Ingredients

- ½ cup spanish rice
- ¼ cup cashews
- 8 oz portobello mushroom
- 1 jalapeño
- 1 lime
- 1 garlic clove
- 1 radish

- 1 scallion
- 1 tbsp liquid smoke
- 1 tbsp tamari
- 4 whole wheat tortillas
- 2 oz shredded red cabbage
- 1 tbsp + 1 tsp vegetable oil
- Salt and pepper

Instructions

- Preheat the oven to 400°F for the tortillas. Place a small saucepan over medium-high heat. Add the Spanish rice, stir, and cook until lightly toasted, about 1 minute. Add 1 cup water and bring to a boil. Cover, reduce heat to low, and cook until all of the water is absorbed and the rice is tender, about 15 to 18 minutes.
- Place the cashews in a small bowl and add ¼ cup hot tap water. Let nuts soak for at least 10 minutes. Thinly slice the portobello mushrooms. Deseed and roughly chop the jalapeño. Peel the garlic. Thinly slice the radish and cut into matchsticks. Thinly slice the scallion. Halve the lime.
- In a blender, combine the cashews and their soaking water, chopped jalapeño, garlic, lime juice, and a pinch of salt and pepper. Blend until smooth.
- Place a large nonstick skillet over medium-high heat with 1 tbsp vegetable oil. Once the oil is hot, add the sliced portobello mushrooms and cook undisturbed until they begin to brown, about 3 to 5 minutes. Add the tamari and just 1 tsp liquid smoke. Toss to evenly coat and cook for an additional 2 to 3 minutes.
- Wrap the tortillas in tin foil and place in the oven to warm, about 3 to 4 minutes. Top the warm tortillas with Spanish rice, smoky portobellos, sliced radishes, sliced scallions, and shredded red cabbage. Drizzle

with jalapeño cashew sauce. Serve smoky portobello tacos with any remaining Spanish rice.

Dinner Spicy Barbacoa Tempeh Recipe

You can make this recipe with Lime Swiss Chard & Avocado.

Serves 2

Prep Time: 10 min

Cook Time: 35 min

Ingredients

- ½ cup short grain brown rice
- 8 oz tempeh
- 1 onion

- 3 cloves garlic
- 6 oz Swiss chard
- 1 avocado
- 1 lime
- 2 chipotle pepper
- 2 tsp Mexican oregano
- 1 tsp ground cumin
- 1 tbsp + 2 tsp apple cider vinegar
- 1 tsp agave
- 2 tbsp vegan sour cream
- 2 tbsp vegetable oil

- Salt and pepper

Instructions

- Add the brown rice, 1¼ cups water, and a pinch of salt to a small saucepan and bring to a boil. Cover, reduce heat to low, and cook until all of the water is absorbed, about 30 to 35 minutes.
- Peel the onion and chop into 1 inch pieces. Peel and mince the garlic. Thinly slice the Swiss chard stems and chop the leaves. Halve the avocado, remove the pit, and thinly slice the flesh. Cut the tempeh into 1 inch cubes. Roughly chop the chipotle peppers.
- Place a large nonstick skillet over medium-high heat with 2 tbsp vegetable oil. Once hot, add the cubed tempeh and cook until golden brown and crisp on most sides, about 4 to 5 minutes. Sprinkle with just half the oregano, season with salt and pepper, and cook for 1 more minute. Transfer cooked tempeh to a plate.
- Return the skillet to medium-high heat and add the chopped onion and minced garlic. Cook, stirring freᐸuently, until softened, about 3 to 5 minutes. Add the chopped chipotle peppers, remaining oregano,

and cumin, and cook until spices are fragrant, about 1 minute. Add the apple cider vinegar, agave, and ½ cup water, and bring to a boil. Reduce heat to low and cook until slightly thickened, about 2 to 3 minutes.

- Return the tempeh to the skillet and turn the heat to high. Cook barbacoa tempeh, tossing frequently, until well coated and browned in places, about 3 to 5 minutes. Transfer the barbacoa tempeh to the plate.
- Return the skillet to high heat and add the Swiss chard, a pinch of salt, and ¼ cup water and cook until wilted, about 2 to 3 minutes. Remove the skillet from the heat. Halve the lime and cut half into wedges. Add the juice from half the lime to the Swiss chard. Divide the brown rice and lime Swiss chard between bowls. Top with barbacoa tempeh, sliced avocado, and sour cream. Serve with lime wedges.

Roasted Red & Green quesadillas Recipe

Serves 2

Prep & Cook Time :30 min

Ingredients

- ½ cup red lentils
- 1 tsp chorizo spice blend
- 4 oz roasted red peppers
- 2 tbsp vegan cream cheese
- 1 avocado
- 2 oz Lacinato kale
- 1 lime

- ¼ cup Follow Your Heart Soy Free Vegenaise
- 2 whole wheat tortillas
- 2 tsp vegetable oil
- Salt and pepper

Instructions

- Add the red lentils, chorizo spice blend, and 1¼ cup water to a small saucepan and bring to a boil. Cover, reduce heat to low and simmer lentils, stirring occasionally, until very tender, about 18 to 22 minutes.
- Drain and finely chop the roasted red peppers. Add them to a medium bowl along with cream cheese and a pinch of salt, mix well with a fork. Halve the avocado and remove the pit. Add the flesh to a separate small bowl. Halve the lime. Add the juice from just half the lime and a pinch of salt to the avocado and mash well with a fork. Destem the kale and thinly slice the leaves.
- Combine the Vegenaise, remaining lime juice, and a pinch of salt in a small bowl. Mix the lime crema.
- Lay the whole wheat tortillas flat on a work surface and spread the red pepper cream cheese on one half, spread the mashed avocado onto the other half. Top with sliced kale. Fold tortillas and press to seal.
- Place a large nonstick skillet over medium heat with 1 tsp vegetable oil. Once the oil is hot, add a quesadilla and cook until golden brown, about 2 to 4 minutes. Carefully flip to brown the other side. Repeat with remaining quesadilla.
- Taste the lentils and adjust the seasoning with salt if necessary.
- Cut quesadillas into thirds and divide between large plates. Serve red and green quesadillas with refried lentils and lime crema for dipping.

The Best Socca Mexican Pizza

Serves 2

Prep & Cook Time: 30 min

Ingredients

- 1¼ cups garbanzo bean flour
- 1 red onion
- ½ cup corn kernels
- ½ tsp chipotle powder
- 1 clove garlic
- ¼ oz fresh cilantro
- 4 oz tomatillo
- 1 jalapeño

- 1 lime
- 13.4 oz black beans
- ¼ cup vegan ranch dressing
- ¼ cup vegan mozzarella
- 2 oz baby arugula
- 2 tbsp + 2 tsp olive oil

- Salt and pepper

Instructions

Step1

- Add the garbanzo bean flour and 1 cup water to a medium bowl and whisk well. Add 1 tbsp olive oil and ⅛ tsp salt. Whisk batter again and set aside until step 4

Step 2

- Set the oven to broil on high. Thinly slice just half of the onion. Add the sliced onion and corn kernels to a baking sheet and toss with 2 tsp olive oil and as much of the chipotle powder as you'd like. Broil until browned in places, about 3 to 6 minutes.

Step 3

- Peel and dice the remaining onion. Peel and mince the garlic. Remove the tomatillo husk and rinse and dice the fruit. Finely chop the cilantro leaves and stems. Trim, deseed, and mince the jalapeño. Combine the diced onion, diced tomatillos, chopped cilantro, minced jalapeño, juice from just half the lime, and a pinch of salt in a medium bowl.

Step 4

- Set the oven to broil on low. Place a large ovenproof skillet over high heat and add 1 tbsp olive oil. Once hot, whisk the batter again, add to the hot skillet, and tilt to cover the entire pan. Cook, undisturbed, until socca begins to bubble, about 4 to 5 minutes. Transfer the skillet to the oven to broil until crisp, about 4 to 6 minutes more.
- Drain and rinse the black beans. Once the socca is browned on the edges, remove from the oven. Spread just half of the ranch dressing over the crust. Top with roasted corn and onions, about half of the black beans, and mozzarella. Return socca pizza to the oven to broil until the cheese melts, about 2 to 4 minutes.

Step 5

- Transfer the socca onto a cutting board and top with tomatillo salsa and baby arugula. Drizzle Mexican Socca Pizza with remaining lime juice and ranch dressing and cut into 6 pieces.
- Enjoy!

Pulled Jackfruit Tacos

Easy recipe with Curtido & Avocado Crema.

Serves 2

Prep & Cook Time: 35 min

Ingredients

- ½ cup red lentils
- 1 onion
- 4 oz shredded green cabbage
- 2 tsp turbinado sugar
- 1 tsp Mexican oregano

- 2 tbsp apple cider vinegar
- ½ oz fresh cilantro
- 1 avocado
- 2 tbsp Follow Your Heart Soy Free Vegenaise
- 1 can organic jackfruit
- 2 tbsp tomato paste
- 1 chipotle pepper in adobo
- 6 corn tortillas
- 2 tbsp vegetable oil
- Salt and pepper

Instructions

- Set the oven to 350°F to warm the tortillas. Combine the red lentils and 1 cup water in a small saucepan over and bring to a boil. Cover, reduce heat to low, and cook lentils until they are very tender and mashable, about 18 to 22 minutes.
- Peel and thinly slice the onion. Add half of the sliced onion to a large bowl along with the green cabbage, Mexican oregano, 1 tsp turbinado sugar, 1 tbsp apple cider vinegar, and a pinch of salt and pepper. Mix curtido with your hands for a minute to break down the cabbage slightly.
- Halve the avocado. In a blender, combine half the avocado, Vegenaise, 1 tsp apple cider vinegar, half the cilantro (stems and leaves), ¼ cup water, and a pinch of salt. Blend the avocado crema until smooth, scraping the sides of the blender as necessary.
- Drain, rinse, and pat the jackfruit dry. Place a large nonstick skillet over medium-high heat with 1 tbsp vegetable oil. Add the jackfruit and remaining sliced onion to the skillet, pulling it apart with your hands, and sprinkle with salt and pepper. Cook, tossing occasionally, until crispy and golden brown in spots, about 5 to 7 minutes.

- Add the tomato paste, remaining turbinado sugar, remaining apple cider vinegar, as much of the chipotle pepper in adobo as you'd like, and ¼ cup water to the skillet. Stir to coat evenly and cook until the jackfruit is crispy, about 3 to 5 minutes. Wrap the corn tortillas in foil and warm them in the oven for about 5 minutes.
- Taste and season the lentils with salt. Slice the remaining avocado. Lay the warmed tortillas onto plates and top with the pulled jackfruit, curtido, and avocado crema. Top with cilantro and sliced avocado. Serve with the lentils.

Poblano Tamale Pie

Delicious recipe with Pinto Beans & Guacamole.

Serves 2

Prep & Cook Time: 35 min

Ingredients

- 2 tbsp vegan butter
- 2 tsp turbinado sugar
- 1 cup masa harina
- 2 poblano peppers
- 4 cloves garlic

- ¼ cup vegan cream cheese
- 1 package pinto beans
- 1 tsp chipotle morita powder
- 1 tomato
- 0.5 oz fresh cilantro
- 1 avocado
- 2 tsp vegetable oil
- Salt and pepper

Instructions

- Preheat the oven to 350°F. Lightly oil a small baking dish with 1 tsp vegetable oil. In a large bowl, combine the butter, turbinado sugar, ½ tsp salt, and 1¼ cups hot tap water and mix well. Add the masa harina, whisk well, and pour the batter into the baking dish. Smooth out the top with a spoon and cover tightly with foil. Bake the tamale dough until it's cooked through, about 20 minutes.
- Deseed and thinly slice the poblano peppers. Peel and thinly slice the garlic.
- Place a large skillet over medium-high heat with 1 tsp vegetable oil. Add the sliced peppers and garlic and a pinch of salt and pepper. Cook, stirring occasionally, until softened and lightly browned in places, about 8 to 10 minutes. Add the cream cheese and 2 tbsp water and reduce heat to low. Simmer until creamy, about 2 to 3 minutes.
- Drain and rinse the pinto beans. Place a small saucepan over medium heat and add the beans, as much of the chipotle morita spice as you'd like, ¼ tsp salt, and 2 tbsp water. Mash some of the beans with a fork and cook until hot, stirring fre?uently, about 3 to 4 minutes.

For guacomale

- Dice the tomato. Pick half the cilantro leaves for garnish, set aside, and roughly chop the remaining leaves and stems. Halve the avocado and remove the pit. Scoop out the flesh, add to a medium bowl, and roughly mash with a fork. Add the diced tomato, chopped cilantro, and a pinch of salt to the avocado and stir the guacamole.
- Cut the baked tamale dough into 4 squares and lay 2 of them onto plates. Top with sauteéd poblanos and another slice of the tamale. Spread with chipotle pinto beans. Top with guacamole and cilantro leaves and enjoy!

Sweet Potato Tacos With Fajita Seasoning & Cilantro Chutney

Serves 2

Prep Time: 10 min

Cook Time: 20 min

Ingredients

- ⅔ cup red lentils
- 1 sweet potato
- 1 red bell pepper
- 2 tbsp fajita seasoning
- 1 seasonal apple

- 3 tbsp cilantro chutney
- 1 lime
- 1 jalapeño
- 3 tbsp vegan sour cream
- 6 white corn tortillas
- 2 oz red cabbage
- 1 tbsp vegetable oil
- Salt and pepper

Instructions

- Preheat the oven to 425°F. Combine the red lentils and 1½ cups water in a small saucepan and bring to a boil. Reduce heat to low. Simmer lentils, stirring occasionally, until they are very tender and mashable, about 18 to 22 minutes. Season with just 1 tbsp of the fajita seasoning.
- Dice the sweet potato (no need to peel). Trim, deseed, and thinly slice the red bell pepper. On a baking sheet, toss the diced sweet potato and sliced bell pepper with 1 tbsp vegetable oil and as much of the remaining fajita seasoning as you'd like. Bake until sweet potatoes are fork-tender and slightly browned, about 18 to 20 minutes.
- Dice the apple. Zest and cut the lime into wedges. Trim, deseed, and mince the jalapeño.
- Add the diced apple, minced jalapeño, just 2 tbsp cilantro chutney, and a pinch of salt to a small bowl. Toss the jalapeño apple slaw to combine.
- In separate small bowl, combine the lime zest, remaining cilantro chutney, sour cream, and pinch of salt. Mix the lime crema to combine.
- Wrap the tortillas in foil and pop in the oven to warm, about 2 to 3 minutes. Divide the tortillas between large plates. Layer on the roasted sweet potatoes and bell pepper and red cabbage. Top the tacos with

jalapeño apple slaw and lime crema. Serve with a side of refried red lentils and lime wedges.

Mushrooms & Green Beans With Vegan Chicken

Serves 6

Prep Time: 10 min

Cooking Time: 30 min

Ingredients

- 1 carrot
- 1 celery stalk
- 1 onion
- 1 garlic clove

- 8 oz oyster mushrooms
- 4 oz green beans
- ½ cup flour
- 1 not chick'n bouillon cube
- 5.5 oz coconut milk
- 1 tsp dried thyme
- ¼ tsp baking soda
- 1 tbsp vegan butter
- 2 tbsp vegetable oil
- Salt and pepper

Instruction

- Peel and dice the carrot. Dice the celery. Peel and dice the onion. Peel and mince the garlic. Trim the oyster mushrooms by removing just the tough ends, about ½ inch. Pull the mushrooms apart. Halve the green beans.
- Place a large nonstick skillet over medium high heat with 2 tbsp vegetable oil. Add just 3 tbsp flour to a large plate with a pinch of pepper and toss the mushroom pieces in it. Once the oil is hot, add the mushrooms in a single layer and cook until lightly browned and crispy, about 2 to 3 minutes per side. Transfer the crispy mushrooms to a paper towel-lined plate and sprinkle with salt.
- For the sauce :Once the mushrooms are finished, reduce the heat to medium (no need to wipe the skillet clean) and add the diced carrot, celery, onion, garlic, and a pinch of salt. Cook, stirring occasionally, until softened, about 4 to 5 minutes. Add the bouillon, coconut milk, dried thyme, and 1 cup water. Bring to a boil, reduce heat to low, and cook until slightly thickened, about 4 to 6 minutes.
- In a large bowl, combine the remaining flour, baking soda, and ¼ cup water. Mix with a fork until well

combined, and drop the dumpling mixture into the simmering sauce by the heaping spoonful. Simmer until the dumplings are firm, about 4 to 5 minutes.

- Add the halved green beans and butter to the chick'n and dumplings and stir gently. Cook until crisp-tender, about 1 minute. Taste and adjust the seasoning with salt and pepper.
- Scoop the chicken and dumplings into large shallow bowls and top with crispy oyster mushrooms.

Pesto Grilled Cheese Recipe

Serves 2

Prep Time: 10 Min

Cooking Time: 20 min

Ingredients

- 1 sweet potato
- 2 tsp dried oregano
- 1 Roma tomato
- 4 slices sourdough bread
- 2 tbsp Follow Your Heart Soy-Free Vegenaise

- ¼ cup vegan basil pesto
- ⅓ cup vegan mozzarella
- ⅓ cup vegan cheddar
- 1 tbsp vegetable oil
- Salt and pepper

Instructions

- Roast the sweet potato fries
- Build your sandwiches
- Cook the pesto grilled cheese
- Serve

Autumn Crunch Salads

Serves 2

Prep & Cook Time: 20 min

Ingredients

- ¼ cup cashews
- 4 oz red grapes
- 1 apple
- 13.4 oz chickpeas
- ¼ cup walnuts
- 1 lemon
- 1 clove garlic

- 2 tsp Dijon mustard
- 1 tbsp white miso paste
- 8 oz kale beet blend
- Salt and pepper

Instructions

- Add the cashews to a small bowl and cover with ¼ cup hot tap water. Halve the grapes. Dice the apple. Drain and rinse the chickpeas.
- Place a small skillet over medium heat and add the walnuts. Toast, shaking the pan occasionally, until the nuts are lightly browned, about 2 to 3 minutes.
- Halve the lemon. Peel the garlic. Add the cashews and their soaking liquid, lemon juice, garlic, Dijon mustard, and white miso paste to a blender. Blend until smooth. Season the creamy cashew dressing to taste with salt and pepper.
- In a large bowl, combine the grapes, diced apple, chickpeas, kale beet blend, a pinch of salt and pepper, and cashew dressing. Divide the autumn crunch salad between bowls and top with walnuts.
- Enjoy!

Penne Mushroom Florentine Recipe

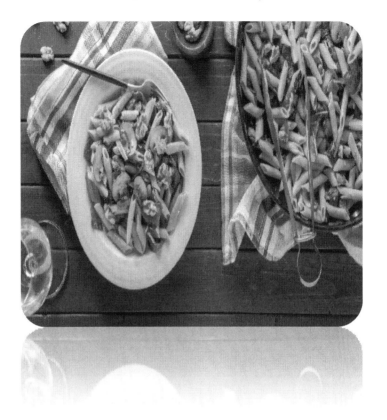

Serves 2

Prep & Cook Time: 30 min

Instructions

- 6 oz cremini mushrooms
- 2 cloves garlic
- 1 shallot
- ¼ cup walnuts
- 8 oz Banza penne
- 2 tbsp vegan butter
- ¼ cup sherry wine

- 1 Not Chick'n Bouillon Cube
- 4 oz baby spinach
- 1 tbsp olive oil
- Salt and pepper

Instruction

- Place a large pot of salted water on to boil for the penne. Thinly slice the mushrooms and wipe clean with a damp towel. Peel and mince the garlic and shallot. Place a large nonstick skillet over medium heat and add the walnuts. Toast, shaking the pan frequently, until fragrant, about 3 to 5 minutes. Transfer toasted walnuts to a plate.
- Return the skillet to medium-high heat with 1 tbsp olive oil. Once hot, add the sliced mushrooms and a pinch of salt and cook, tossing occasionally, until browned in places, about 3 to 5 minutes. Add the minced garlic, shallot, and a pinch of salt and pepper, and cook until softened, about 2 to 4 minutes.
- Add the penne to the boiling water. Cook, stirring occasionally, until al dente (or slightly undercooked), about 3 to 5 minutes. Reserve 1 cup of pasta water. Drain the penne and rinse with cold water. Add the butter to the skillet with the mushrooms, increase the heat to high, and add the cooked penne. Cook, stirring occasionally, until browned in places, about 3 to 5 minutes.
- Add the sherry wine to the skillet and cook for 1 minute. Whisk the Bouillon cube into the reserved pasta water and add to the skillet. Bring to a boil and cook until slightly thickened, about 2 to 3 minutes. Add the baby spinach to the skillet and toss until wilted, about 1 to 2 minutes.
- Divide the penne mushroom florentine between large shallow bowls and top with toasted walnuts.

Ancient Grain Bowl

Serves 1

Total Time: 1 hr

Ingredients

Bowl

- 1 1/2 tbsp farro
- 1 1/2 tbsp quinoa
- 1 tbsp dried garbanzo beans

- 1 carrot
- 1/4 tsp sesame oil
- pinch of salt & pepper, Italian seasoning
- 1 bunch dandelion green
- 1/2 tsp sesame oil, pinch of salt & pepper, 1/2 tsp turmeric
- 1 radish, thinly sliced
- 1/2 avocado
- 1 heaped tbsp hummus
- Parsley pesto
- 1 cup curly parsly
- 1/2 lemon
- 1/4 cup cashews
- 1/3 cup sunflower seeds
- 1 tbsp nutritional yeast
- 1/2 tsp salt
- 3 tbsp extra virgin olive oil

Instructions

- Soak farro, quinoa and garbanzo beans in filtered water over night.
- When ready to cook, rinse a few times. Then add about 1 cup of water and boil for about 20 minutes until everything (including the chick peas) are soft.
- Preheat the oven to 390 Fahrenheit. Wash and slice the carrot, drizzle with sesame oil, salt & pepper and Italian seasoning. Roast in the oven for about 15 minutes.
- Wash and cut dandelion greens into shorter chunks.
- Heat sesame oil over medium heat in heavy pan, then add dandelion greens, salt & pepper and turmeric. Cook until soft.
- For the pesto place all ingredients into the food processor until coarse.

- Arrange grain mix into a bowl, then add dandelion greens and carrots, sliced radish and avocado. Add a good dallop of pesto as well as hummus.

☐

Stone Fruit Salad With Avocado

Serves 2

Total Time: 35 min

Instructions

- 1 oz fresh ginger
- 1 garlic clove
- ¾ cup beluga lentils
- ½ tsp ground coriander
- 6 oz green Swiss chard
- 1 avocado
- 1 fresh peach
- 2 tbsp hazelnuts

- 1 tbsp Champagne vinegar
- ¼ cup dried tart cherries
- 1 tbsp + 2 tsp olive oil
- Salt and pepper

Instructions

Toast the aromatics

- Peel and mince the ginger and garlic. Rinse and sort the lentils. Place a small saucepan over medium heat with 2 tsp olive oil. Once hot, add the minced ginger, garlic, and coriander, and cook, stirring frequently, until spices are fragrant, about 1 minute.
- Cook the lentils -Add the lentils and 1¼ cups water to the saucepan and bring to a boil. Cover, reduce heat to low, and cook until the lentils are tender and water is absorbed, about 15 to 20 minutes. Season the lentils with salt.
- Thinly slice the Swiss chard stems and chop the leaves. Halve the avocado and remove the pit. Thinly slice the flesh. Working around the pit, dice the peach. Roughly chop the hazelnuts.
- Add the Swiss chard stems and leaves to a large bowl. Add the Champagne vinegar and a pinch of salt and pepper, and toss, gently massaging the greens with your hands, for 1 minute.
- Add the cooked lentils, chopped hazelnuts, dried tart cherries and 1 tbsp olive oil to the bowl with the swiss chard. Gently toss, taste, and adjust seasoning with salt and pepper. To serve, divide the warm lentil salad between large, shallow bowls. Top with sliced avocado and diced peaches.

Baked Mango Cauliflower Wings Recipe

Servings 2

Total Time: 40 min

Ingredients

- 10 oz potatoes
- 1 cup flour
- 1 tsp smoked paprika
- 1 head cauliflower
- 2 tbsp vegan butter
- ½ cup hot sauce
- 2 tsp Sriracha
- ¼ cup mango chutney

- 1 carrot
- 2 celery stalks
- ¼ cup High Omega Vegan Bleu Cheese
- 1 tbsp vegetable oil
- Salt and pepper

Instructions

- Preheat the oven to 425°F. Peel and chop the potatoes and add them to a small saucepan. Cover with 1 inch of water, bring to a boil, and cook until just tender, about 10 to 12 minutes. Drain potatoes and transfer to a large bowl.
- Add the flour, smoked paprika, 1 cup water, and ½ tsp salt in a large bowl and whick to combine. Trim and cut the cauliflower into small florets. Add the cauliflower florets to the bowl with the batter and toss well. Coat a baking sheet with 1 tbsp vegetable oil and transfer the cauliflower to the baking sheet, shaking off any excess batter. Bake until crispy, about 18 to 20 minutes.
- Place a medium saucepan over medium heat and add the butter, hot sauce, Sriracha, and mango chutney. Cook the mango hot sauce, stirring often, until hot, about 2 to 3 minutes.
- Peel and dice the carrot into ½ inch cubes. Dice just 1 celery stalk and cut the remaining stalk into 3 inch pieces for dipping. Add the diced carrots and diced celery to the potatoes with just half the bleu cheese dressing and a pinch of salt and pepper. Toss bleu cheese potato salad to evenly coat.
- Once finished, add the baked cauliflower to the saucepan with the mango hot sauce and toss to coat (you may have to work in batches). Using a slotted spoon, transfer the mango cauliflower back to the

baking sheet and bake until sticky, about 3 to 5 minutes more.
- Divide the baked mango cauliflower wings between large plates serve with the bleu cheese potato salad and celery sticks. Serve with remaining bleu cheese dressing for dipping.

Chickpea Sandwiches With Garlic Roasted Carrot Fries

Serves 2

Total Time: 30 min

Ingredients

- 4 carrots
- 1 tsp garlic powder
- 1 shallot
- 1 lemon
- 13.4 oz chickpeas

- ¼ oz tarragon
- 3 tbsp Follow Your Heart Soy Free Vegenaise
- 2 oz baby arugula
- 2 tbsp capers
- 2 ciabatta bread
- 2 tbsp olive oil
- Salt and pepper

Instructions

- Preheat the oven to 425°F. Peel the carrots and cut into 4 inch long sticks (you want a fry shape). Add to a baking sheet and toss with 2 tsp olive oil, garlic powder, salt, and pepper. Bake fries until tender and brown in places, about 10 to 15 minutes.
- Peel and mince the shallot. Halve the lemon. Drain, rinse, and dry the chickpeas and add to a large bowl. Pull the tarragon leaves from the stems by running your thumb and first finger down the stem.
- In a blender, combine 2 tbsp lemon juice, tarragon leaves, Vegenaise, just half of the baby arugula, and a pinch of salt and pepper. Blend green goddess dressing until smooth.
- Mash the chickpeas with the back of a fork. Add the minced shallot, green goddess dressing, and capers to the mashed chickpeas and stir to combine. Taste and adjust the seasoning with salt and pepper as necessary.
- Halve the ciabatta rolls lengthwise, brush each half with 1 tsp olive oil, and place in the oven to toast, about 3 to 4 minutes.
- Spread the green goddess chickpea salad onto two toasted ciabatta halves. Top with the remaining baby arugula. Serve with a side of garlic roasted carrot fries.

☐

Avocado quinoa Burger With Kale Recipe

Serves 2

Total Time: 35 min

Ingredients

- ¼ cup Quinoa
- 13.4 oz chickpeas
- 1 avocado
- 1 clove garlic
- ¼ cup Forager Project Cashewgurt
- 2 tbsp Soy-Free Vegenaise
- ¼ cup panko breadcrumbs
- 1 tsp chipotle morita powder
- 8 oz Kale Beet Blend

- 1 tbsp champagne vinegar
- 2 tbsp vegetable oil
- Salt and pepper

Instructions

- Cook the Ɋuinoa :Add the quinoa, ½ cup water, and a pinch of salt to a small saucepan over high heat. Bring to a boil, reduce heat, cover, and cook until the spirals burst and all of the water is absorbed, about 10 to 12 minutes.
- For garlic dressing ;Peel and mince the garlic clove. In a medium bowl combine the minced garlic, Cashewgurt, Vegenaise, and a pinch of salt and pepper, and mix the garlic dressing well. Drain, rinse, and dry the chickpeas. Halve the avocado, remove the pit and dice the flesh.
- Add just ½ cup of chickpeas, cooked Ɋuinoa, panko breadcrumbs, chipotle morita powder, and ½ tsp salt to a food processor. Blend until well combined, scraping down the sides as necessary. Add the burger mixture to a large bowl, and fold in half of the diced avocado.
- Divide the burger mixture in half and press firmly to form four patties, each about ¾ inch thick. Place a large nonstick skillet over medium-high heat with 2 tbsp vegetable oil. Once hot, add the avocado Ɋuinoa burgers and cook until crispy and warmed through, about 5 to 7 minutes per side.
- Add the kale beet blend to the rinsed large bowl with the remaining chickpeas, just 2 tbsp garlic dressing, Champagne vinegar, a pinch of salt and pepper. Toss the kale beet slaw.
- Divide the kale beet slaw between large plates and top with avocado Ɋuinoa burgers. Top with remaining

diced avocado and serve with remaining garlic dressing.

Cavatappi With Asparagus & Carrot Pesto

Serves 2

Total Time: 30 min

Ingredients

- 8 oz carrots
- 10 oz asparagus
- 2 cloves garlic
- 1 lemon
- 1 box Banza cavatappi
- ⅓ cup almonds
- 4 oz baby arugula

- ¼ cup soy free vegan parmesan
- 1 tsp + 2 tbsp olive oil
- Salt and pepper

Instructions

- Preheat the oven to 400°F. Bring a large pot of salted water to a boil for the pasta. Peel and thinly slice the carrots. Trim about 1 inch off the tough asparagus ends and chop the stalks into 1 inch pieces. Peel the garlic.
- Add the sliced carrots to a baking sheet and toss with 1 tsp olive oil and a pinch of salt and pepper. Roast until fork-tender, about 10 to 12 minutes.
- Measure out 1 cup of the cavatappi and save for another use. Add the remaining cavatappi to the boiling water and stir. Reduce heat slightly and cook until al dente, about 6 to 8 minutes. Reserve ½ cup of the pasta water and drain the pasta.
- Halve the lemon. Combine the roasted carrots, garlic, juice from just half the lemon, almonds, just ½ cup of arugula, 2 tbsp parmesan, ¼ tsp salt, and ¼ cup water in a food processor. Pulse until well combined. With the motor running, drizzle in 2 tbsp olive oil and blend carrot pesto until smooth.
- Return the large pot to medium-high heat with 2 tsp olive oil. Add the chopped asparagus and cook until crisp-tender, about 2 to 3 minutes. Add the cooked cavatappi, reserved pasta water, carrot pesto, remaining lemon juice, remaining arugula, and cook, stirring gently, until the arugula is slightly wilted, about 1 to 2 minutes. Taste and adjust seasoning with salt and pepper.
- Divide the carrot pesto cavatappi between large shallow bowls and sprinkle with remaining parmesan.
- Enjoy !

□

Easy Thai Peanut Sauce

This peanut sauce is the perfect sauce for salads, spring rolls, noodles, and more!

Total Time: 10 min

Serves 2

Ingredients

- 1/4 cup natural peanut butter
- 2 tbsp sesame oil

- 2 tbsp soy sauce
- 1 tbsp rice vinegar
- 2 tsp fresh ginger, peeled and grated
- 1-2 cloves garlic, minced
- 1 tsp maple syrup
- juice of 1/2 lime
- pinch of cayenne
- 2 tbsp water, as needed

Instructions

- Using a Microplane, grate the ginger and set aside.
- In a small bowl, combine all the ingredients EXCEPT the water. Using a whisk or an immersion blender, whisk the ingredients together until a thick, uniform sauce is formed.
- Add water, as needed, until you have reached desired consistency.

- Serve immediately with spring rolls or over salad or noodles. Store in an airtight container in the refrigerator for up to 5 days.

Quick, Simple & Spicy Udon Recipe

Prep Time: 10 minutes

Cook Time: 30 minutes

Servings : 2

Ingredients

- 1 tablespoon coconut oil
- 1 onion, diced
- 2 cloves garlic, minced
- 1 cm (1/2 inch) ginger, peeled and minced

- 1 heaped teaspoon curry powder, to taste
- 1 teaspoon ground cumin
- 1 teaspoon ground turmeric
- 1 carrot, peeled and sliced
- 4/5 cuptinned tomatoes
- 4/5 cup coconut milk
- 1 vegetable stock cube
- 1 teaspoon agave syrup
- 1 tablespoon tamari
- 1 tablespoon cornflour (cornstarch)
- Salt + pepper, to taste
- 3 portions udon noodles

Instructions

- Heat up the coconut oil in pan and add onion, garlic and ginger once hot
- Fry for about 10 minutes until softened
- Add curry powder, cumin and turmeric and fry for a minute until fragrant
- Add the carrots, tinned tomatoes, coconut milk, stock cube, agave syrup and tamari, with 600ml (2 1/2 cups) water
- Bring to the boil then turn down heat and simmer for 15-20 minutes
- Dissolve the cornflour in a small amount of water in a separate bowl, before adding to the curry
- Stir well and leave to heat gently for a further couple of minutes until sauce is thickened. If it's still looking too thin, do the same with more cornflour dissolved in water first - or add more water
- Add salt + pepper to taste
- Meanwhile, cook the udon noodles according to instructions on packet

- Place the cooked noodles in bowls and pour over the curry soup

Thai Salad Made With Sesame Oil

Total Time: 10 min

Serves: 8

Ingredients

- 1/4 cup almond butter
- 1/4 cup coconut milk canned (full fat)
- 1/4 cup rice wine vinegar unseasoned, plain
- 1 tablespoon sesame oil

- 3 tablespoons coconut aminos sub 1 tablespoon soy sauce if desired
- 1 tablespoon lime juice fresh
- 1-2 teaspoons sriracha hot sauce
- 2 teaspoons honey or sub date syrup
- 1/4-1/2 sea salt to taste

Instructions

- Add all ingredients (omitting the sea salt), starting with 1 teaspoon of sriracha (unless you know you love it spicy), to a blender. Blend well for 1-2 minutes, until mixture begins to lighten and looks well mixed (the coconut milk will make it get slightly "fluffy."
- Taste, and adjust seasonings to taste. Add more lime or sriracha if you love those flavors, and use a dash of sea salt to bring the flavors out more if desired.
- Store in the refrigerator for up to 4 days. Coconut milk does go bad ⁇uickly, so this dressing isn't something you can have around for a long time.
- If you'd like the dressing to be "pourable," bring it to room temperature and stir well before serving. The oils in the almond butter and coconut milk will softly solidify when refrigerated.

Sesame Lotus Root Recipe

Total Time: 20mins

Serves: 2

Ingredients

- ½, a whole lotus root sliced very thinly
- 1 piece fresh ginger, peeled and chopped (about 1 inch long)
- 2 garlic, cloved peeled and chopped

- 1 1/2 cups of roughly chopped green onions
- 2 tablespoons hot red chili peppers, finely chopped
- oil vinegar for the lotus root water
- 1 tablespoon sesame seeds
- pepper
- 1 1/2 tablespoons soy sauce
- 1 teaspoon sesame oil

Directions

- Put the sliced lotus root into vinegar water as you slice it, as described above. Drain well just before cooking.
- Heat up a large frying pan with the oil. Add ginger and garlic, and stir fry until the oil is very fragrant.
- Add the drained lotus root slices in a single layer. Cook until the lotus root slices start to change color - they turn a bit translucent looking. Turn over and cook a couple more minutes.
- Add the chili pepper and green onions, and stir-fry. Add the sesame seeds, pepper, soy sauce and sesame oil.
- The lotus roots should get a bit caramelized from the soy sauce. Serve hot or cold. This is very nice for bento.

Banh Mi Wraps With Kimchi & Teriyaki Tofu

Serves: 2

Total Time: 5 min

Ingredients

- 7 oz Wildwood Organic Sproutofu Baked Teriyaki Tofu
- ¼ oz fresh cilantro
- 2 tsp Sriracha
- ¼ cup Follow Your Heart Soy-Free Vegenaise
- 2 flour tortillas

- 4 oz shredded carrots
- 2 oz vegan cabbage kimchi

Instructions

Prepare the wraps

- Small dice the tofu. Roughly chop the cilantro leaves and stems.
- In a small bowl, combine the Sriracha and Vegenaise. Lay the tortillas out flat and top with diced tofu, chopped cilantro, shredded carrots, and kimchi. Drizzle with Sriracha Vegenaise.
- Fold in the sides and wrap tightly.

Sushi Bowl, Tofu & Cucumber Recipe

serves: 2

Prep & Cook Time: 5 min

Ingredients

- 8 oz rice and ⯑uinoa vegetable blend
- 6 oz Wildwood Organic Sproutofu Baked Tofu
- 1 cucumber
- 2 oz baby spinach
- 1 cup edamame

- ¼ cup Follow Your Heart Organic Miso Ginger dressing
- 2 oz pickled ginger

Instructions

For the bowls

- Make a small 2 inch tear in the top of the rice and quinoa vegetable blend bag, and microwave for 1 minute. Cut the tofu into cubes. Thinly slice the cucumber. Add the rice quinoa vegetable blend to a large bowl and toss with the spinach, edamame, and miso ginger dressing.
- Divide the salad between 2 bowls.
- Top with the tofu, cucumber, and pickled ginger.
- Enjoy!

Lemony Braised Chickpeas With Scallion Cashew Cheese

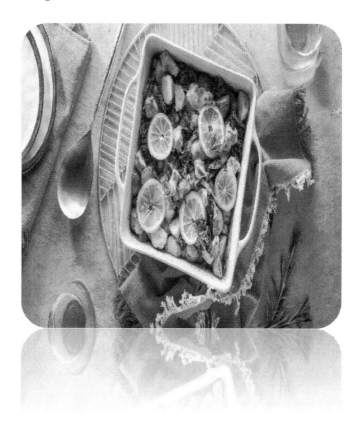

Serves 2

Total Time: 40 min

Ingredients

- 1 onion
- 2 cloves garlic
- ¼ oz fresh rosemary

- 1 oz kalamata olives
- 13.4 oz chickpeas
- 10 oz red bliss potatoes
- 2 tbsp nonpareil capers
- 4 oz curly kale
- 2 lemons
- 2 oz Treeline scallion cashew cheese
- 4 tbsp + 2 tsp olive oil
- Salt and pepper

Instructions

- Preheat the oven at 450°F. Peel and thinly slice the onion. Peel and mince the garlic. Pick the rosemary leaves from the stems. Halve the kalamata olives. Drain and rinse the chickpeas. Cut the red potatoes into quarters (no need to peel).
- Place a medium saucepan over medium-high heat with 1 tsp olive oil. Add the sliced onion, minced garlic, and a pinch of salt and pepper, and cook until softened, about 3 to 4 minutes. Transfer the onions and garlic into a baking dish.
- Add chickpeas, capers, rosemary, olives, potatoes, 4 tbsp olive oil, ¼ cup water, and a pinch of salt and pepper to the baking dish with the onions and garlic. Stir to combine. Cover tightly with foil and bake until the potatoes are tender, about 20 to 25 minutes.
- Desteem the kale and thinly slice the leaves. Return the saucepan to medium-high heat with 1 tsp olive oil. Add the sliced kale and cook until bright green and wilted, about 2 to 4 minutes.
- Thinly slice one of the lemons into rounds. When the chickpeas are finished, remove the foil and add the kale and toss. Turn the oven to broil on high. Crumble the scallion cheese onto the braised chickpeas and top

with the sliced lemon. Broil until the cheese is lightly browned, about 2 to 3 minutes.

- Halve the remaining lemon. Squeeze the remaining lemon over the baking dish. Serve the lemon braised chickpeas with rosemary straight from the baking dish, family style.
- Enjoy!

Roasted Carrot Hummus Bowl With Tahini & Carrots

Serves 2

Total Time: 30 min

Ingredients

- 8 oz carrots
- 1 zucchini
- 2 garlic cloves
- 1 lemon
- 1 tbsp za'atar seasoning

- 13.4 oz cannellini beans
- 2 tbsp tahini
- 1 grilled flatbread
- 4 oz baby arugula
- 2 oz Treeline Scallion Cashew Cheese
- 1 oz red peppadew peppers
- 3 tbsp olive oil
- Salt and pepper

Instructions

- Preheat oven to 425°F. Peel the carrots and slice on the diagonal. Trim and roughly chop the zucchini. Peel the garlic. Halve the lemon.
- Transfer the sliced carrots to a baking sheet and toss with 2 tsp olive oil, just half the za'atar, and a pinch of salt and pepper. Roast until tender and blackened in spots, about 14 to 16 minutes.
- Place a large nonstick skillet over medium-high heat with 1 tsp olive oil. Once hot, add the chopped zucchini and cook, tossing occasionally, until tender and charred in places, about 3 to 5 minutes. Sprinkle vegetables with salt and cover with foil to keep warm.
- Drain and rinse the cannellini beans. Add the roasted za'atar carrots, garlic, just 2 tbsp lemon juice, just half of the beans, tahini, and ½ tsp salt to a food processor. Pulse to combine, then with the motor running, drizzle in 2 tbsp olive oil and 2 tbsp water, blending until smooth. Taste the roasted carrot hummus and adjust seasoning with salt.
- 5 Finishing touches
- Pop the flatbread into the oven to toast, about 5 to 7 minutes. Remove from the oven and cut into 8 triangles. Add the arugula to a medium bowl and toss with any remaining lemon juice and a pinch of salt and pepper.

- Spread the roasted carrot hummus on the bottom of large shallow bowls or plates.
- Top with arugula salad, sautéed zucchini, and remaining cannellini beans. Dollop bowls with Scallion Cashew Cheese and sprinkle with peppadews and remaining za'atar.
- Enjoy with warm flatbread.

Tabouli Mezzi Bowls With Sweet Pea Hummus & Grilled Bread

Serves 2

Total Time: 30 min

Ingredients

- 2 rainbow carrots
- 1 tsp ground sumac
- 13.4 oz cannellini beans
- 1 lemon

- 2 garlic cloves
- 1 shallot
- ¼ oz fresh mint
- ½ cup green peas
- 1 grilled flatbread
- 7 oz Cedar's Tabouli
- 2 tsp vegetable oil
- 4 tbsp olive oil
- Salt and pepper

Instructions

- Preheat oven to 425°F. Peel the carrots and cut into 2 inch long sticks. Transfer to a baking sheet and toss with 2 tsp vegetable oil, ground sumac, and a pinch of salt and pepper. Roast the carrots until tender and browned on the bottom, about 12 to 15 minutes.
- Drain, rinse, and dry the cannellini beans. Zest and halve the lemon. Peel and mince the garlic. Peel and thinly slice the shallot. Pick the mint leaves from the stems.
- Add just ½ cup cannellini beans, lemon zest, just half of the minced garlic, sliced shallot, 2 tbsp olive oil, and a pinch of salt and pepper to a small bowl. Stir to combine and let the beans marinate until plating.
- Add the remaining cannellini beans, lemon juice, remaining garlic, mint leaves, green peas, 2 tbsp olive oil, and a pinch of salt and pepper to a food processor. Blend until smooth, about 2 to 3 minutes.
- Pop the flatbread into the oven to toast, about 5 to 7 minutes. Remove from the oven and cut into 8 triangles. Divide the tabouli between bowls. Serve alongside the sumac roasted carrots, marinated cannellini beans, and mint pea hummus. Enjoy with the warm flatbread.

☐

Hummus Bowls With Stuffed Grape Leaves & Whole Wheat Pita

Serves 2

Total Time: 5 min

Ingredient

- 4 radishes
- 4 oz roasted red peppers
- 2 whole wheat pita
- 4 oz green beans
- ½ cup Kalamata olives

- 4 brown rice stuffed grape leaves
- 4 oz hummus

Instructions

- Check the olives for pits and remove if present. Thinly slice the radishes. Drain the roasted red peppers. Quarter the pitas. When you're ready to eat, divide the radishes, roasted red peppers, green beans, stuffed grape leaves, hummus, and olives between 2 serving bowls, serve with pitas.

Socca Tart With Summer Squash

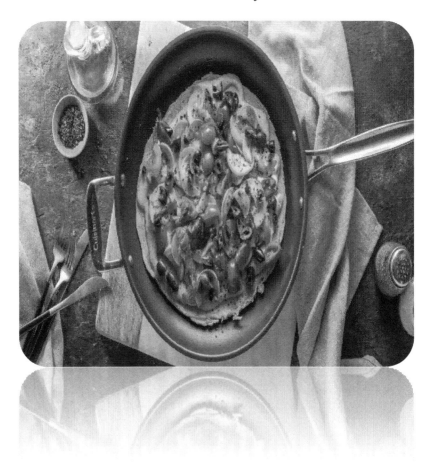

Serves 3

Prep Time: 10 min

Cook Time: 25 min

Ingredients

- 1¼ cups garbanzo bean flour
- ¼ cup kalamata olives
- 1 clove garlic

- 1 lemon
- ⅓ cup cashews
- 1 summer squash
- 4 oz cherry tomatoes
- 2 oz Treeline Scallion Cashew Cheese
- 2 tbsp nutritional yeast
- 2 tsp red chile flakes
- 1 tbsp + 2 tsp olive oil
- Salt and pepper

Instructions

- Step 1, In a medium bowl, combine the garbanzo bean flour and 1 cup of water, whisk well. Add 1 tbsp olive oil and ⅛ tsp salt. Whisk batter again and set aside until step 4.
- Step 2, Check the Kalamata olives for pits and remove if present. Roughly chop the olives. Peel and mince the garlic. Halve the lemon. Place the cashews in a small bowl and add 1/4 cup hot water. Let soak for at least 10 minutes.
- Step 3, Trim the summer squash and cut into half moons. Halve the cherry tomatoes. Place a large nonstick oven-safe skillet over medium-high heat with 2 tsp olive oil. Once the oil is hot, add the cut summer squash and cherry tomatoes, and a pinch of salt and pepper. Cook, tossing occasionally, until browned in places, about 5 to 7 minutes. Transfer the vegetables to a bowl.
- Step 4, Add 2 tbsp lemon juice, the cashews and their soaking water, Scallion Cashew Cheese, nutritional yeast, garlic, ¼ tsp salt, and ¼ tsp pepper to a blender. Blend the cashew sauce on high until smooth. Taste and adjust seasoning with salt and pepper.

- Step 5, Set the oven to broil on low. Return the skillet to high heat and add 1 tbsp olive oil. Once hot, whisk the batter again, add to the hot skillet, and tilt to cover the entire pan. Cook, undisturbed, until socca begins to bubble, about 4 to 5 minutes. Place the skillet in the oven and broil until crisp, about 4 to 6 minutes.
- Transfer the socca crust to a cutting board. Spread the cashew sauce on the crust. Top with sauteéed summer squash and cherry tomatoes. Sprinkle with chopped olives and as many red chile flakes as you'd like. Enjoy!

Greens & Grains Bowl With Lemon Tahini

Serves 2

Total Time: 25 min

Ingredients

- 6 oz Swiss chard
- 3 scallions
- ½ cup walnuts
- 1 clove clove garlic
- 1 lemon

- 2 tbsp tahini
- 6 oz precooked Quinoa
- 3 tbsp hemp seeds
- 2 oz roasted tomatoes
- 4 tsp olive oil
- Salt and pepper

Instructions

- Thinly slice the Swiss chard stems and roughly chop the leaves; keep separate. Thinly slice the scallions.
- Place a large nonstick skillet over medium heat with the walnuts. Cook until toasted and fragrant, about 3 to 5 minutes. Transfer nuts to a bowl and set aside.
- Peel and grate the clove of garlic over a medium bowl. Add the tahini, juice from half the lemon, and 2 tbsp warm water. Whisk until you have a smooth dressing, adding more water as necessary. Season lemon tahini with salt and add more lemon juice if necessary.
- Return the nonstick skillet to medium-high heat with 2 tsp olive oil. Once hot, add the chard stems and cook for 1 to 2 minutes. Add the leaves and ¼ cup of water to create some steam. Cook the chard until bright green and just wilted, about 1 to 3 minutes more. Season greens with salt and pepper.
- Make a small tear on either side of the quinoa bag, and microwave for 60 seconds. Empty quinoa into a bowl and add 2 tsp olive oil, the sliced scallions, and hemp seeds. Season with salt and pepper.
- Divide the chard and quinoa between large bowls. Top bowls with roasted tomatoes, toasted walnuts, and lemon tahini. Serve with any remaining lemon.

Quinoa Power Bowls With Chickpeas & Stuffed Grape Leaves

Serves 2

Total Time: 5 min

Ingredients

- 6 oz precooked quinoa
- 13.4 oz chickpeas
- 4 brown rice stuffed grape leaves
- ½ oz fresh dill

- ¼ cup dried tart cherries
- ¼ cup lemon vinaigrette

Instruction

- Make a 2 inch tear in the top of the quinoa bag and microwave for 1 minute. Drain and rinse the chickpeas. Roughly chop the grape leaves. Roughly chop the dill fronds.
- Divide the quinoa between two serving bowls. Top with chickpeas, chopped grape leaves, dill, and dried cherries. When you're ready to eat, drizzle with lemon vinaigrette.

Mediterranean Skillet With Tzatziki Cucumber Salad

Serves 2

Total Time: 35 min

Instructions

- ½ cup farro
- 2 vegan apple sage sausages
- 2 cloves garlic
- 1 shallot

- 2 mini sweet peppers
- 13.4 oz chickpeas
- ¼ oz fresh dill
- 1 cucumber
- 1 lemon
- ¼ cup vegan yogurt
- 3 tbsp olive oil
- Salt and pepper

Instructions

- Add the farro to a small saucepan and cover with cold water (the water should be at least 1 inch over the farro). Bring to a boil, reduce heat to low, and cook until the grains are tender, about 15 to 18 minutes. Drain any excess water.
- Remove the apple sage sausage from the wrapper and thinly slice into rounds. Place a large nonstick skillet over medium-high heat with 1 tbsp olive oil. Add the sausage and cook, stirring occasionally, until browned and crispy, about 5 to 6 minutes. Transfer the crispy sausage to a plate.
- Peel and mince the shallot. Peel and mince the garlic. Trim, deseed and mince the mini sweet peppers. Return the skillet to medium-high heat with 2 tbsp olive oil. Add the minced shallot, just half the minced garlic, and a pinch of salt and pepper and cook until the shallot is softened, about 2 to 3 minutes.
- Drain and rinse the chickpeas. Add the chickpeas, cooked farro, and diced peppers to the skillet and season with salt and pepper and toss well. Cook until the farro is crispy in places, about 3 to 4 minutes.
- Chop the dill fronds. Thinly slice the cucumber. Halve the lemon. Combine the chopped dill, sliced cucumber, yogurt, remaining minced garlic, juice from just half the lemon, and a pinch of salt and

pepper in a medium bowl. Toss the tzatziki cucumber salad.

- Cut the remaining lemon into wedges. Top the skillet with the apple sage sausage and cook until hot. Divide the Mediterranean skillet between plates and serve with the tzatziki cucumber salad and lemon wedges. Enjoy!

Mediterranean Stuffed Sweet Potatos

This recipe is made with Crispy Chickpeas & Scallion Cashew Cheese.

Serves 2

Total Time: 35 min

Ingredients

- 2 sweet potatoes
- 13.4 oz chickpeas
- 1 tbsp ras el hanout
- ½ cup quinoa

- 1 lemon
- 1 scallion
- 4 oz roasted red peppers
- ¼ cup walnuts
- ¼ tsp ground cumin
- 1 tbsp balsamic glaze
- 1 cucumber
- 2 oz Treeline scallion cashew cheese
- 3 tbsp + 2 tsp olive oil
- Salt and pepper

Instructions

- Preheat the oven to 425°F. Poke a few holes in the sweet potatoes with a fork, slice them lengthwise, and transfer to one half of a baking sheet. Rub potatoes with 1 tsp olive oil each and sprinkle with a pinch of salt and pepper.
- Drain and rinse the chickpeas. Pat dry with a paper towel and add to the other side of the baking sheet with the sweet potatoes. Toss the chickpeas with 1 tbsp olive oil, ras el hanout, and a pinch of salt and pepper. Bake until the chickpeas are crispy and the sweet potatoes are tender, about 30 to 35 minutes.
- Add the ⵁuinoa, ¾ cups water, and a pinch of salt to a small saucepan and bring to a boil. Cover, reduce heat to low, and cook until the water is absorbed and the grains are tender, about 12 to 15 minutes.
- Halve the lemon. Roughly chop the scallion. In a blender combine juice from just half the lemon, roasted red peppers, the chopped scallion, walnuts, cumin, just 1 tbsp balsamic glaze, and 2 tbsp olive oil. Blend on high until smooth and season with salt.
- Dice the cucumber. Cut the remaining lemon into wedges. Once the sweet potatoes are done, flip and mash the flesh slightly with a fork.

- Divide the quinoa between large plates and top with roasted sweet potatoes. Layer on the crispy chickpeas, roasted red pepper vinaigrette, diced cucumbers, and scallion cashew cheese. Serve with lemon wedges.

Crispy Quinoa Cakes With Red Pepper Artichoke Antipasto & Ranch Dressing

Serves 2

Total Time: 30 min

Ingredients

- ½ cup Quinoa
- 2 tbsp flaxseed meal
- 1 shallot

- 2 cloves garlic
- 1 can artichoke hearts
- ¼ oz fresh parsley
- 1 romaine heart
- 1 cup panko breadcrumbs
- 4 oz roasted red peppers
- 1 tbsp red wine vinegar
- ¼ cup Follow Your Heart High Omega Vegan Ranch
- 1 tbsp + 1 tsp olive oil
- 1 tbsp vegetable oil
- Salt and pepper

Instructions

- Add the Quinoa, 1 cup water, and a pinch of salt to a small saucepan and bring to a boil. Cover, reduce heat to low, and cook until the spirals burst and all of the water is absorbed, about 10 to 12 minutes.
- In a small bowl, whisk together the flaxseed meal and 5 tbsp water. Peel and roughly chop the shallot and garlic. Drain the artichoke hearts and Quarter. Pick the parsley leaves and tender stems. Halve the romaine heart lengthwise.
- Add the cooked quinoa, flaxseed mixture, chopped shallot, garlic, panko breadcrumbs, and a pinch of salt and pepper to a food processor. Pulse until combined, scraping the sides of the food processor with a spatula as necessary. Form the quinoa mixture into 6 half-inch thick cakes.
- Place a large nonstick skillet over medium-high heat with 2 tsp olive oil. Once the oil is hot, add the romaine, cut side down, and press down with a spatula. Cook until charred in places, about 2 to 3 minutes. Transfer to a plate and season with salt and pepper.

- Return the skillet to medium-high heat with 1 tbsp vegetable oil. Add the ⍰uinoa cakes and cook until browned, about 2 to 3 minutes per side. Add the ⍰uartered artichoke hearts, parsley, roasted red peppers, red wine vinegar, and 2 tsp olive oil to a medium bowl. Season antipasto with salt and pepper and toss.
- Lay the charred romaine on large plates and drizzle with just half the ranch dressing. Top with the crispy quinoa cakes and red pepper artichoke antipasto. Serve with remaining ranch dressing.

Chapter 5: Plant-Based Snack Recipes

Matcha Energy Bites

Serves 4

Total Time: 20 min

Ingredients

- 2 cups rolled oats

- 1 tbsp matcha powder
- ¼ cup maple syrup
- ¼ cup cashew butter
- 1 banana
- ½ cup dried blueberries

Instructions

- In a food processor, pulse the oats and matcha powder until the oats are coarsely ground. Peel and add the banana, maple syrup, cashew butter, and a pinch of salt. Blend until a dough forms and transfer to a large bowl. Mix in the dried blueberries.
- Roll the mixture into 12 round balls and chill in the refrigerator.

Peach Ginger Crips

Serves: 2

Total Time: 1 hr

Ingredients

- 3 lbs fresh peaches, peeled and sliced
- 2 tbsp minced ginger
- 1 ½ cups all-purpose flour, separated
- ½ cup light brown sugar, separated
- ½ cup rolled oats
- 6 tbsp vegan butter, chilled

- ¼ cup marzipan
- ¼ cup sliced almonds

Instructions

Filling

- Preheat the oven to 350°F. Add the sliced peaches, minced ginger, just 2 tbsp of the flour, just ¼ cup of the sugar, and a pinch of salt to a large bowl and toss. Toss the peaches every few minutes to ensure an even coating until you're ready to bake.
- Almond topping
- In another large bowl, mix together the remaining flour, brown sugar, oats, sliced almonds, and ⅛ tsp salt. Add the butter and marzipan and mix the mixture with your hands, squeezing with your fingers, until a crumbly dough forms.

Bake

- Pour the filling into an 8 x 8" baking dish and top with the almond topping. Bake in the oven until lightly browned, about 40 to 45 minutes. The peaches should be bubbly, you may need to place a baking sheet under the dish to avoid dripping. Let the cobbler rest 15 minutes before scooping and serving with plant-based vanilla ice cream.

Cashew Cheesecake

Serves 4

Prep & Cook Time :40 min active + 5 hrs in freezer

Ingredients

- 1½ cups raw cashews
- 1 cup Medjool dates
- 1 cup raw walnuts
- ¼ tsp salt
- ⅓ cup coconut oil

- 1 13.5-oz can coconut cream
- ½ cup maple syrup
- 2 tsp vanilla extract
- 1 lemon
- Any toppings of choice. Ex, melted vegan chocolate, candied citrus, or fresh fruit

Instructions

- Add the cashews to a saucepan and cover with 1 inch water. Bring to a boil, reduce heat to medium, and simmer until softened, about 25 to 30 minutes. Once ready, drain and set aside (they can soak until you're ready to blend).
- Line a springform pan with parchment paper. Remove the pits from the dates. Add the pitted dates, walnuts, and salt to a food processor. Pulse until the mixture is well combined. Empty the walnut-date mixture into the springform pan and press to evenly coat the bottom. Let the walnut-date crust set in the freezer for 1 hour.
- Combine the soaked cashews, coconut oil, coconut cream, maple syrup, vanilla extract, and the juice from the lemon in a blender. Blend until smooth.
- Pour the blended cashew mixture into the walnut-date crust. Cover cashew cheesecake with plastic wrap and return to the freezer to set, at least 4 to 5 hours. Once cheesecake is firm to the touch, top with melted vegan chocolate, candied citrus, or garnish with fresh fruit.
- Slice and enjoy!

Fruit & Coconut Popsicle Recipe

Serves 4

Total Time: 10 min + freezing time

Ingredients

- 2 limes
- 13 oz coconut milk (large can)
- 3 tbsp agave
- 2 cups fresh mixed berries, halved if large

Instructions

Zest and halve the limes.

- In a large bowl, combine the lime zest, lime juice, coconut milk, agave, and fresh berries. Mix well and pour into popsicle molds. Freeze overnight or for at least 4 hours. Serve on a hot summer day!

Pumpkin Pie

Serves 4

Prep Time: 15 min

Cooking Time: 1 hr

This version of pumpkin pie has all of the fall flavor you've been craving: vanilla, cinnamon, cloves, nutmeg, and, of course, pumpkin! Be sure to buy an "unspiced" pumpkin puree.

Ingredients

- 1 tbsp coconut oil
- 2 cups all-purpose flour
- 2 tbsp granulated sugar
- ¼ tsp salt
- 6 tbsp cashew milk
- 5 tbsp vegan butter (chilled)
- 2 cups pumpkin puree
- 1 tsp vanilla
- 3 tbsp cornstarch
- 2 tsp pumpkin pie spice
- ¼ cup brown sugar
- 1 tbsp maple syrup
- Optional: vegan ice cream for serving

Instructions

- Preheat the oven to 350°. Grease a pie pan with coconut oil. Add the flour, granulated sugar, ¼ tsp salt, and cashew milk to a food processor. Blend on low until the combined. Add the cold butter 1 tsp at a time until the dough is wet and starts to stick together. Press the dough into the pie pan, covering the bottom and the sides. Bake until golden brown, about 20 to 25 minutes. Remove from the oven and let cool.
- Filling -In a large bowl, add the pumpkin puree, vanilla, cornstarch, pumpkin pie spice, brown sugar, and maple syrup. Mix until smooth. Pour the filling into the baked crust, and spread evenly with a spatula or back of a spoon.
- Bake the pumpkin pie for 25 to 30 minutes, until browned. Serve the pie warm or chilled in the fridge with a side of your favorite vegan ice cream. Enjoy!

Falafel Recipe

Serves 4

Total Time: 20 min

Ingredients

- 1 small yellow onion
- ½ cup parsley leaves
- 2 cloves garlic
- 1 tsp ground cumin
- 1 tsp ground coriander

- 1 cup garbanzo bean flour
- 3 tbsp olive oil

Instructions

- Peel and roughly chop the onion. Add the onion, parsley leaves, garlic, ground cumin, ground coriander, and ¾ tsp salt to a food processor. Pulse until well chopped. Add the garbanzo bean flour and ¼ cup water. Blend until a cohesive dough forms.
- Form the falafel dough into 6 two-inch patties. Place a large nonstick skillet over medium-high heat with 3 tbsp olive oil. Once hot, add the falafel and cook until browned and crisp, about 3 to 4 minutes per side. Sprinkle each with salt.
- Serve falafel with your favorite toppings! We like pita, sliced tomatoes, onions, cucumber, and our recipe for lemon yogurt.

Sweet & Salty Coconut Chips

Serves 4

Prep Time: 5 min

Cook Time: 15 min

Ingredients

- 3 cups coconut flakes
- 1 tablespoon coconut oil
- 3 tablespoons agave
- 1/2 teaspoon sea salt

Instructions

- Prep: Preheat oven to 350. Line a baking sheet with parchment paper. Melt the coconut oil for 30 seconds in the microwave or on a pan over low heat for 1 minute, set aside.
- Add the dried coconut flakes to a large mixing bowl and set aside.
- Combine the agave, melted coconut oil and 1/2 teaspoon sea salt in a small bowl, mix thoroughly.
- Add the sauce to the coconut flakes and mix to combine.
- Spread the coconut mixture on a baking tray, bake for 10 minutes.
- Remove from the oven, stir, and return to the oven and bake to get coconut chips crispy, but not burned, about 5 minutes. Set aside to cool, and enjoy!

☐

Cinnamon Sugar Pita Chips

Serves 4

Prep & Cook: Time 15 min

Ingredients

- 2 pocketless pitas
- 1 tbsp coconut oil, melted
- 1 tbsp cane sugar
- 2 tsp ground cinnamon
- 1 ripe peach
- 1 tbsp minced red onion
- 1 tbsp white balsamic vinegar

- 2 tbsp fresh tarragon leaves
- 1 minced Thai chile

Instructions

- Preheat the oven to 400°F. Line a baking sheet with foi. Cut the pitas into wedges and transfer to a baking sheet. Lightly brush both sides with melted coconut oil. Mix sugar and cinnamon together in a small bowl and sprinkle on both sides of the pita wedges. Bake chips until golden brown and crispy, about 5 to 8 minutes.
- Remove the pit from the peach and small dice the flesh. In a medium bowl, combine the diced peach, minced red onion, white balsamic vinegar, and picked tarragon. Add Thai chile if you like it hot. Enjoy!

Fresh Fruit Salad with Yogurt

Any variety of fruit could be used in this fresh fruit salad. Great for a party or after dinner treat, this simple salad should be tossed with the yogurt right before serving

Serves 4

Total Time : 10 min

Ingredients

For the fruit salad

- 1 large organic watermelon
- 1 organic canary or honeydew melon

- 1 organic pineapple
- 1 cup organic blueberries
- 1 pint organic strawberries
- For the honey-mint dressing
- 1 pint organic yogurt
- 3-4 tablespoons organic raw honey (adjust to taste)
- 2 tablespoons organic chopped mint leaves

Instructions

- Dice the melons, or use a melon baller to shape them into bite-sized pieces.
- Wash and dice the strawberries and pineapple and toss them with the melon. Add the blueberries and stir once more.
- In a bowl, mix the ingredients for the honey-mint yogurt.
- Serve the yogurt on the side, or toss the salad with it if you prefer.

Chapter 6: Plant-Based Grill Recipes

Garlic & Balsamic Smoky Mushrooms

What you need:

- 1 kilogram mushrooms, sliced into 1/4-inch thick pieces
- 3 cloves garlic, chopped
- 2 tablespoons balsamic vinegar
- 1 tablespoon soy sauce

- 1/2 teaspoon thyme
- Salt and ground black pepper to taste

Directions

- Mix together garlic, balsamic vinegar, soy sauce and thyme in a bowl. Season with salt and pepper. Place mushrooms in the bowl and toss to coat with marinade. Cover and refrigerate for at least 30 minutes. When ready, thread mushrooms onto skewers and cook on a pre-heated grill over medium-high heat for 2 to 3 minutes per side or until tender.

Grilled Potatoes With Creamy Lemon Dressing

What you need:

- 3/4 kilogram baby white potatoes, boiled and sliced in half
- 2 lemons, juiced
- 2 cloves garlic, minced
- 2 onions, chopped
- 1 cup fresh cilantro leaves
- 1 cup fresh Italian parsley leaves
- 6 tablespoons olive oil, plus more for brushing
- 1 teaspoon salt, plus more for seasoning

- 1/4 teaspoon black pepper, plus more for seasoning

Directions

- Brush boiled baby potato halves with olive oil then season with salt and pepper. Cook on a pre-heated grill over medium high heat, cut side down for 10 minutes. Transfer to a serving plate. Combine lemon juice, garlic, onion, cilantro, parsley, olive oil, salt and pepper in a blender. Blend until mixture is smooth. Serve as dipping sauce or over grilled potatoes.
- These amazing plant-based grill recipes are great to pair with your grilled meat!

Grilled Tropica Tofu

What you need:

- 1 pineapple, sliced into rings
- 3 lemons, squeezed
- 1 block firm tofu, pressed and sliced into triangle filets
- 3 tablespoons fresh pineapple juice
- 1 tablespoon brown sugar
- 2 teaspoons tamari
- 1/4 teaspoon turmeric
- Handful of cilantro
- Coconut oil

Directions

- In a dish, mix together lemon juice, pineapple juice, brown sugar, turmeric, tamari and cilantro. Whisk to combine ingredients well.
- Arrange tofu filets on top of marinade. Using a tong, carefully flip over filets to coat the other side with marinade. Marinate for at least 4 hours.
- When ready, brush tofu with coconut oil and cook on a pre-heated grill over medium high heat for 20 minutes. Flip and grill for 10 more minutes.
- Remove from the heat then grill pineapple rings until nice grill marks appear, about 5 minutes. Serve tofu topped with a pineapple ring.

Chapter 7: Plant-Based Smoothie Recipes

Creamy Dragon Fruit Smoothie Bowl

Total Time: 10 minutes

Serves: 2

Ingredients

- 1 large white fleshed Dragon Fruit or a purple fleshed Dragon fruit
- 1 cup plain yogurt
- 1 cup milk of choice
- 1 large banana
- 1 tablespoon honey
- fresh blackberries
- fresh blueberries
- 1 tablespoon slivered almonds
- 1 tablespoon granola

Directions

- Cut and peel the Dragon fruit and place in a blender with the yogurt, milk, banana, and honey.
- Pulse until well combined.
- Divide into two bowls.
- Top with blackberries, blueberries, almonds and granola.

Avocado Banana Green Smoothie Bowl With Blueberries

Total: 10 min

Serves: 1

Ingredients

- 1/2 of avocado
- 2 cups fresh baby spinach
- 1/2 medium-size banana
- 1 small peach
- 1 tablespoon peanut butter

- 2 tablespoons rolled oats
- about 1.35 fl oz coconut water (or regular water)

TOPPING (Optional)

- Blueberries (amount depends on your taste)
- one teaspoon of cacao nibs

Directions

- Add all smoothie ingredients to a blender. Blend on high until you reach smooth and creamy consistency.
- Pour everything into a bowl. Add topping ingredients.
- Enjoy your Avocado Banana Green Smoothie Bowl!

Healthy Green Smoothie Bowl

Total Time: 35 minutes

Serves: 2

Ingredients

- 1 medium-size ripe banana (about 4 oz.), sliced
- 2 cups frozen chopped spinach (about 5 oz.)
- 1/2 cup fresh pineapple cubes (about 2 1/2 oz.)
- 1/2 cup coconut water, plus more as needed
- 2 small kiwis (about 5 1/2 oz.), peeled and chopped

- 2 tablespoons hempseed Pinch of salt 2 teaspoons chopped fresh ginger, optional
- 1/2 teaspoon raw honey, optional Desired toppings

Directions

- Freeze banana slices for at least 30 minutes or up to 1 day.
- Place banana, spinach, pineapple, coconut water, kiwis, hempseed, salt, and, if desired, ginger and honey in a blender; process until smooth, 20 to 30 seconds, stopping to stir and scrape down sides as needed. (If mixture is too thick, add up to 4 tablespoons coconut water and process again.) Divide between 2 bowls and sprinkle with toppings.
- Serve immediately.

☐

Golden Milk Smoothie

Total Time: 5 minutes

Serves: 2

Ingredients

- 1 cup banana(ripe, sliced, and frozen)
- 1 cup light coconut milk or almond milk
- 1/2 tsp ground turmeric

- 1 Tbsp fresh ginger (plus more to taste)
- 1 Dash ground cinnamon
- 1 Dash black pepper
- 1 Dash ground nutmeg
- 1 Dash ground clove and cardamom
- 1/4 cup fresh carrot juice

For Serving(optional)

- 1 Tbsp Hemp seeds

Directions

- Add banana, coconut milk, turmeric, ginger, cinnamon, black pepper, and nutmeg to a high-speed blender and blend on high until creamy and smooth. If including, add cardamom, clove, and fresh carrot juice at this time (optional).
- If too thick, thin with more coconut milk or water. If too thin, thicken with ice (or more frozen banana, though it will add more sweetness).
- Taste and adjust flavor as needed, adding more cinnamon for warmth, black pepper for spice, ginger for "zing," turmeric for earthiness / more intense color, or banana for sweetness. Adding carrot juice will also add sweetness and more intense orange/yellow hue.
- Divide between serving glasses (ours are from West Elm) and enjoy immediately. Keep leftovers in the refrigerator for 24 hours.
- Freeze leftovers by pouring into an ice cube tray and use for future smoothies (either this smoothie or others you'd like to infuse with a golden milk flavor).

Blueberry Almond Smoothie

Serves 1

Total Time 5 mins

Ingredients

- 1 banana, peeled
- 1 cup frozen blueberries
- 1/2 cup almond butter
- 1/2 cup plain yogurt
- 3/4 cup almond milk
- 3 dates, pitted and quartered
- 1 cup ice, or as needed

Instructions

- Combine all ingredients in a blender; purée on high speed until smooth.
- Add a few ice cubes and blend until it reaches your desired consistency.

Enjoy a healthy happy life ☺ !

Printed in Great
Britain
by Amazon